The Strength In Knowing

THE TRUTH BEYOND OUR BELIEF SYSTEMS, AND A FRESH PATH FINDING LOVE, PEACE, AND JOY

I. Alan Appt

HBP

Hartford & Baines Publishers

Charleston South Carolina

ISBN-13: 978-0-9895224-0-3
ISBN-10: 0989522407

Library of Congress Control Number: 2012909971

Hartford & Baines Publishers
Charleston, South Carolina

Printed and bound in the United States of America

PRAISE FOR
THE STRENGTH IN KNOWING

"*The Strength in Knowing* is a heartfelt depiction of one man's journey to spiritual enlightenment and self-discovery. This book will be a wonderful read for those who are beginning to search for more meaning, love and direction in their lives. The author suggests several valuable and realistically attainable ways to begin one's path to a more fulfilling, joyful and God-centered journey on the physical plane."

Thomas S. Lipsitz, PhD
Clinical Psychology, Saint Louis Missouri

"*The Strength in Knowing* is truly inspirational reading, enriching and thought provoking. The world would be a dramatically better place if even a few of us would be guided by its powerful ideas. The busier you are, the more revelations you will find."

Anthony S. Shen, M.D.
Missouri Baptist Medical Center

"When your thinking is unlimited, so is your potential. Appt, and his new awareness, is a true emergence and unveiling where he explores and identifies the specific skills you need to make your potential for success explode into results."

Nadim Nasrallah, M.S. D.C. M.A.
Saint Louis Missouri

Contents

DEDICATION

De gratia Dominus illuminatio mea
By favor of grace, the lord is my light

Foreword

Faith is the turning of the body, mind, and spirit to God in an intimate way. Faith is an act of communing with God that most commonly takes the form of adoration, contrition, thanksgiving, and supplication or petition. In *The Strength in Knowing*, I. Alan Appt will teach you how to think in a way that will keep you ahead in these turbulent times and create exciting opportunities and possibilities. The book will take you places you've never been before and get you to think in ways you've never thought before.

Awareness is also a process of orienting ourselves toward God in a way that reveres God's almighty power and goodness and habituates us to look to God. Yet awareness also, perhaps even more so, guides us to look within ourselves for everything.

Appt's life experience is manifested in his writing, and his writing will show you that you cannot change your life until you change things you do daily. When your thinking is unlimited, so is your potential. Appt's new awareness is a true revelation, and Appt will explore and identify the specific skills you need to make your potential for success explode into results.

The content of this book is the fruit of Appt's many life experiences, high and low. The material is aimed toward preparing people not only for the difficult times that may lie ahead, but also for the era of peace of mind and peace of heart in finding oneself. This book assists the reader step by step to make the journey from the head to the heart. By exploring and analyzing yourself, you will enable a better tomorrow and enjoy the real fullness of life. Unless a person consciously strives to go counter-culture, it is impossible to experience such a change until you battle against yourself. In reading the various sections of this book, try to keep the faith. Faith is often birthed out of difficulties; allow yourself to explore faith if you are experiencing difficulties.

This book can help you approach life after good or bad times with a completely new perspective. The truth and power ring deep in every sentence. *The Strength in Knowing* leads the way to find our best and highest place within our self, with the hope and intent of a true transformation.

Appt's book is an exceptional one that promises to make a positive difference in our lives. It will engage you and demonstrate to you how people can live with integrity using self-awareness and beliefs as guidelines, regardless of religion, culture, or circumstance.

Nadim Nasrallah, M.S. D.C. M.A.
Saint Louis, Missouri

Author's Preface

For many years, I have asked myself why premonitions, spiritual and intuitive events, were occurring in my life. Perhaps the reason was and is the purpose of the book. I never mentioned the incidents that had occurred to anyone until recently. I suspect it was the fact that I was afraid to tell others about the experiences, because of the incredible content.

Most recently, I have felt an insatiable need and an intense passion to write this book. I never dreamed of writing a book until now. A portion of the inspiration for my book came from the awareness realized from one of my teachers, Master Luong Minh Dang, my very good friend Paymon Ghasedi, and Charles Dahlheimer.

I felt a tremendous need to convey what I have learned to others as a result of spiritual events, intense meditation, and ensuing heightened awareness that have occurred in my life. In addition, I have undergone an extensive education in studies directly relating to existentialism, consciousness, spirituality and meditation. It is my wish that the experiences mentioned earlier might help others construct a more comprehensive understanding of their own lives and existences.

When I began the book, I somehow found myself writing thoughts I did not know and yet seemed to know. It was almost as though I had some sort of guidance besides my own consciousness relating to knowledge of certain philosophical and psychological subjects.

I mentioned to my wife, Pam, on many occasions that, at certain times, I felt I was writing the words but the words written were flowing from another source. It was knowledge I never learned, but somehow I knew.

I feel that my spiritual practices and experiences, in conjunction with an open mind, have enabled me to have a heightened self-discovery, understanding, and awareness. In addition, some of my unexplained awareness may conceivably be the result of knowledge from a past life.

I am not a trained philosopher or psychologist, but I am a fundamentally spiritual and religious person who has had many astounding experiences and realizations. I believe these experiences and realizations may help others to see a bigger purpose, significance, and understanding about their lives and existence.

Where did I come from? What am I? Where am I going? With many books written on the subject, this one directly relates to mostly empirical knowledge rather than postulated thought. What I have experienced, learned, and realized in my life that may spiral ones belief system from subjective subject matter to an actual knowing.

A belief system we may have, like religion that perhaps transformed into an actual reality, a knowing. If we can attain an actual truth through knowing, then perhaps at some juncture we will have reached that realization. When, the realization is accomplished, we will have gone beyond or supplemented our belief systems with pragmatic knowledge.

We are exploring a more comprehensive understanding of emotional states of mind, consisting of, fear, guilt, and anger, to name a few. I will address and place a significant emphasis on love with a greater appreciation and awareness of attitude and its importance in everyday living.

An understanding of duality and its effects on our daily lives, like good and evil, love and hate. A narrative of a means conceivably transcending to a non-dual state of mind, an enlightened state of being.

A greater understanding of spirituality, the eternal through meditation, derived awareness, and empirical knowledge, in a language that is easy to absorb. I will discuss these topics and my experiences and awareness of events throughout the book.

I have had many spiritual events occur in my life—one event in particular, which happened in 1987, was the impetus for my book. A synopsis of the experience is as follows. I will go into more detail later about many other spiritual events.

I was living with my first wife at our home in St. Louis County, Missouri.

It was early one evening, and I had been in bed reading for about an hour. I was perhaps twenty-five or thirty feet from the bathroom door.

Suddenly, through my peripheral vision, I thought I saw something on the bathroom door. When I looked up, I could not believe my eyes: there was a vision on the door. It was the face of what looked like a man with a mustache and a beard, slightly longer than a goatee. The vision was full size and depicted the man's head, neck, and shoulders. He had some sort of cloth wrapped around his forehead and tied at the back. He also had stringy, shoulder-length hair.

I could not move a bone in my body; my eyes were locked onto whatever this was. As I continued to stare, white and blue particles about the size of pinheads began swirling just below the man's neck area. It seemed as though the more I stared, the more lifelike the image became. I had a sense that the colored particles were enhancing the image's development. I could not recall how much time had elapsed, but I suspected a matter of a few minutes or less.

My wife walked into the room and started talking to me. The second she started talking, the vision gradually began to diminish. I suppose I had a choice whether to tell her what was happening, but I chose to say nothing. In less than a minute, the vision was nearly gone. Finally, she finished talking. I responded with a belated reply, and she left the room. I jumped out of bed and ran to the door. I had to touch the door, although I don't know what I expected to find. The image was gone, and the door appeared to be normal, with a very slight white outline of what had been there. I touched it, and within a matter of a few seconds, it was gone. My recollection of this event is as though it happened yesterday.

During that experience, I asked myself why I was seeing the apparition. Who was I seeing? What did it mean? The first time I asked myself these questions, the answers that popped into my head were. I felt that I was seeing Jesus. But if so, why? I am Jewish, but so was Jesus and a rabbi too.

Did this mean I was going to die? Alternatively, was the world ending? Was I destined to do something significant in my life, perhaps for mankind? These were the thoughts that entered my mind at the time.

I did not die, and the world did not end. For years off and on, I thought about this incredible event—this overwhelming and indescribable experience. I somehow feel there are not words to describe how I felt then, and what occurred afterward.

This book is an attempt to convey to others what I have learned and experienced in the hope that they may have a better understanding and appreciation of life's purpose and meaning. I hope to enrich their lives and perhaps give them a peace that is so essential in a fulfilled existence.

Acknowledgements

I would like to acknowledge my wife Pamela Appt, who I am blessed to have in my life. She enthusiastically encourages me and provides never-ending inspiration and support.

Without Pam, this book would not be possible.

INTRODUCTION

Writing this book has been an unbelievable experience for me. I have been able to express so much I have held inside for so long. Some of what I discuss consists of personal firsthand examples from my own life. I wrote a large amount of the book from 10:00 in the evening until about 3:30 in the morning. I virtually always seem to have a deeper insight at this time and find the words flow much easier.

A key aspect of *The Strength in Knowing* is it enables the reader at virtually any age to recognize how short life is and understand the urgency in finding one's own truths. Our origin and our destiny are subjects discussed for a comprehension of the self and our relation to others. Readers will gain a stronger awareness of how ego reduction can enable love, peace, and joy to surface. The ego, being the nemesis of our true fulfillment, can thus be redirected.

I strive to address any negative and environmental indoctrination, associations, and belief systems we may maintain and implement methods for improvement. The book emphasizes the importance of predominantly utilizing veracity, as opposed to perception, in our lives. It offers a deep insight into why bad things happen to good people and children. The book encourages meditation techniques for finding balance, sensitivity, knowledge and for manifesting our desires in life.

The Strength in Knowing helps us realize our capacity to recognize true romantic love in our lives, ultimately uncovering and addressing the existence of fallacious relationships. It also helps us to recognize the importance of addressing relevant plateaus regarding age in relation to our desires.

I present a brief explanation and evaluation of cause and effect, destiny, energy, the time-space continuum, and the concept of time actually passing faster. I stress how essential it is for people to remain in the present and discuss how to avoid dwelling on negative aspects of the past. Helping you see how finding a path to realizing a higher level of consciousness is fundamental for true fulfillment. In addition, guiding you on the road to finding purpose, the meaning of existence, and ultimately, true happiness.

With peace,
I. Alan Appt

SECTION I

Pursuit of Awareness

Chapter 1

The Beginning

I suppose it all began when I was ten or eleven years old, that is, this sense of a need to have answers about life's purpose and my purpose. I engaged in a lot of existential thought for my age, or perhaps for any age. I still, to this day, do not know what possessed me to be so interested in existentialism, as young as I was. Have you ever thought about where we came from? What are we, that which is called a human being? Where are we going? I do not mean the fact that we originated from our mothers' wombs. Childbirth is a result of the act of making love. However, how did the act of making love to perpetuate childbirth originate? From Adam and Eve? In addition, are we anything else besides human beings, with our intelligence and physical presence? Where are we going on our journey, and what does life really mean?

Processes and evolution enable the acts and methods we have learned and utilized. As, people grow and with age, they gain empirical knowledge. Nevertheless, where did the processes and techniques that we now know about originate? What am I, besides this identification as a human being with what we call a flesh-and-bone body—the intelligent life-form that each of us is and this physical entity that evolves? What is our purpose—do we have a purpose? What is our ultimate destiny? Where are we going when we depart the planet? Though those questions were phrased differently at the time of my youth, I do not suppose young as I was, that I realized that the questions I pondered had such a tremendous amount of philosophical depth.

I recall arriving home from school when, rather than playing, I felt a desire to go to my room. I picked up a piece of paper and began writing. I do not recall what the impetus was to begin writing; I can only suspect it had something to do with my life's purpose. What I wrote was a poem, and it began like this:

To Be
To be for me to be is to be.
And to be is being and being
Is to be. Therefore so shall I be.

A friend of my mother, named Beth, was visiting; my bedroom door was open, and she walked in. She asked what I was doing, and I replied, "Oh, just writing." She asked if she could see what I was writing, and I replied, "Sure." She read the poem and looked at me with the most peculiar expression. She said the poem was nice, but I did not understand the meaning of her expression for some time. If I was able to correctly identify the look she had, it was most likely astonishment at the content of the poem. I suspect she wondered how the poem could be so profound when written by someone so young.

Nothing of any significance, with respect to my inquisitive nature, occurred again for some time, that I can recall. I believe it wasn't until several years later, when I was in my early teens that anything unusual occurred.

I returned to this philosophical state periodically, asking the proverbial questions: who am I, where did I come from, and where am I going? These thoughts I do not believe ever left my mind from the time of the poem "To Be." I was plagued with these questions and found myself feverishly reading books relating to existentialism. I had hoped that they would give me the answers I needed. At times, as I continued with this pursuit, I would become mentally overwhelmed with my identity issue. I became very anxious and somewhat depressed, as the exploration seemed to overload my brain. I felt like my problems were similar to those of a computer when it could not digest data because of the unusual volume or the complexity of the content. The computer may become overloaded and end up crashing, or perhaps shorting out due to the lack of a circuit breaker. I felt, at times, that I might be losing touch with reality. There were actually periods of time when I did not understand who I was.

I knew that I was this entity described as a human being. I knew my name and the other essential aspects of my nature, and I had all the functions we normally possess, but somehow that knowledge was not enough. It seemed as though there was an awareness that was lacking in my consciousness that was crucial to my identity issue. I find it extremely difficult to describe exactly how I felt then. It was almost as though my brain was able to comprehend my state of mind, but I was unable to formulate a description of how I actually felt because the way I felt was indescribable. I had a sense of knowing, but it was just an inexpressible feeling. Why could I not simply accept the fact that I was an intelligent life form called a human being and leave it at that? Was I attempting to find answers to questions that perhaps did not have any answers?

I became frightened and tried not to think anymore about the subject. The answers I needed were difficult for me to comprehend because of my inability to discern that which, perhaps, I might never know about existentialism. The answers given in the books I read were subjective, stemming only from authors' observations and their understanding. The philosophical aspect of virtually anything may stem from one's own perception rather than resulting from scientific documentation. So deductions based on knowledge or values, logical reasoning, and critical analysis of fundamental assumptions or beliefs about a subject would then be based strictly on perception, rather than on pragmatic evidence.

Continually plagued with my identity issue for about six months in my mid-twenties, I sought psychological help, which at first I was not certain would be beneficial. The help was therapy for despair, I suspect, because of my anxiety and inability to resolve my identity issue. Despondency accompanied this state of mind. Where did I come from, what was I, and where was I going? My inability to understand these aspects of my existence was becoming overwhelming for me. In addition, during some of these uncertain periods, I felt I was actually beginning to lose touch with reality. On rare occasions, I also had thoughts of suicide, either by taking some sleeping pills or by crashing my car into a tree off the side of the road. I do not believe the suicidal thoughts would ever have come to fruition, but the fact that I had them was very disturbing to me just the same. I believed and realized that the thought of the loss of my life should be God's decision and not mine, regardless of the circumstances.

As much as therapy does, sometimes it causes one to look at questions and concerns from a different perspective. Somehow, when another person poses questions or makes statements, it perpetuates a different approach to a better understanding of the subject. Therapy would help me find reasons and answers for some of my questions.

But ultimately, we in essence answer most of our own questions and concerns in the course of therapy. The therapist's expertise in knowing when to ask the proper questions and when to make the necessary statements facilitates success for the patient. The therapy and the accompanying medication helped me reduce the fear and despondency with which I had been plagued. This, in turn, enabled me to find a greater acceptance of that which is, was, and shall be. However, the acceptance was still not enough of an explanation or understanding for me. I continued to struggle to comprehend the questions that still plagued me: where did I come from, what am I, and where am I going?

Occasionally when an individual is in a low emotional state, a level of anxiety may catapult him or her to a higher state of being. Perhaps this higher state of being or awareness may even extricate the person from a state of depression and into a more normal state of mind or even a higher level of consciousness. Many times, states of depression, anxiety, and ruin can be stages in life by which some of us may be elevated to higher states of mind or even states of change.

Devastation can be a reward and a path to regeneration.

Let us compare anxiety and depression, which are low points in one's life, to throwing a football or baseball. The thrower's arm is lowered behind him or her in order to obtain the greatest height and distance. In shot put or javelin competition, the competitor bends to the lowest position in order to obtain the greatest height or distance. Anxiety or depression may be the low points or the vehicles, *on occasion*, that transform us to higher mental states or states of change.

We are sometimes able to free ourselves from negative states such as alcoholism or drug abuse with programs specifically tailored for this. I believe that these programs may be supplemented or accomplished with this type of viewpoint. *When the intensity it takes to extricate one from a negative state is equal to or greater than the intensity that perpetuated the state, then the person can be freed of that state.* The application of this process for depression or other conditions is appropriate when the individual has an extreme commitment to success. I say "process," but I mean that which would require concentrated focus and willpower to facilitate release from a negative state. An intense commitment to success is key to and fundamental for extricating oneself from the negative situation.

Sometimes people do not have the will and motivation for a cure. In some instances, this might be due to a fear of facing reality or of facing situations one just does not want to deal with. Another instance might be when someone needs attention, usually because of his or her current state of mind or despondency. The original process I mentioned to extricate oneself from the negative state, may require therapy to facilitate, first, the inspiration and motivation necessary to enable the essential concentration needed to accomplish the cure. The situation, mental pain, and degree of dysfunction of the individual would dictate the degree of focus required for success.

Understanding the ingredients that brought this state of mind or level of pain to the present status is paramount and essential. If we search our hearts, souls, and minds for answers to why we are who we are, the answers are there, waiting to be brought to the surface.

We must permit ourselves to access the truth from the deep abyss it dwells in, in spite of the pain the truth may produce. Success for the individual is based on an awareness of the causes of a problem coupled with the proper focus, dedication, and trust in God that will ultimately make possible the release. If therapy is necessary, it may reveal the aspects of the personality that brought about the negative state, if one isn't successful in identifying by them self. And again, if treatment is necessary, and if it is accompanied by a strong enough will for success through intense focus and dedication and trust in God, it will unequivocally generate freedom from that which plagues the individual.

The purity of all that is, an awareness of the divine in the entire splendor of what exists is expressed in the devotion of one's ability to discern the eternal (without a beginning or end.)

SUMMARY OF BELIEF SYSTEMS

1) The philosophical aspect of virtually anything may be one's perception rather than the result of scientific documentation.

2) Analysis of fundamental assumptions or beliefs about a subject would strictly involve perception rather than pragmatic evidence.

3) If we have a stronger awareness and appreciation of what we possess, it will ultimately enable greater peace for us.

4) One should search their heart, soul, and mind for the answers to why you are who you are.

5) If identification of our own causes of negative states of mind is unsuccessful, therapy may be necessary.

6) It is essential to know the ingredients that brought these states of mind or levels of pain to the present status.

7) One must focus in order to access the truth, regardless of how painful it might be.

8) Success for the individual is based on an awareness of the causes, coupled with the proper focus, dedication, and trust in God that will ultimately make possible the release.

9) Many times, states of depression, anxiety, and ruin can be stages in life that elevate us to higher states of mind or states of change.

10) If the intensity needed to extricate one from a negative state is equal to or greater than that which perpetuated the state, then one can be free of that state.

11) This particular process would require intense focus and willpower to facilitate release from a negative state.

12) Intense commitment to success is fundamental for one's extrication from the negative situation.

13) Inspiration and motivation are necessary to enable the essential strength needed to accomplish the goal.

14) Intense focus, dedication, and trust in God will unequivocally generate freedom from that which plagues us.

Chapter 2

Physical Awareness

I know I have a body and that it consists of flesh and bone. The body has things called organs, blood, veins, cells, arteries, and much more, all of which facilitate bodily functions. The body has five senses, and of course it contains the unbelievable brain with its extraordinary abilities. All of our bodily functions and organs operate according to their own specific purposes and maintain a flawless excellence—all of the organs joined in an absolute synchronicity of perfection that so many take for granted. However, most of all, the body contains a *life force*, in addition to all of those components, that can be explained less by physiological means than by spiritual. We have a life force that makes living things alive. It ignites all the components and enables *life*, which allows the body to function and perform all its requirements. Could all of this specificity of perfection have occurred spontaneously or by accident? Who are we, besides our physical bodies?

The Latin *Cogito Ergo Sum*, translated, as *"I think; therefore I am,"* is a quote from the French philosopher Rene Descartes. The meaning of the phrase is that if someone contemplates whether or not he or she exists, something has to exist, in and of itself, to have enabled the question to be thought in the first place. If we can think and have consciousness, we therefore must exist as living entities with intelligence and with the ability to differentiate. Yet somehow, this explanation was not entirely sufficient for me. It only validates the fact that someone exists with a consciousness. It does not give any definitive answer to questions about life, purpose, and meaning.

Consciousness is the ability to reason, to discern, and to comprehend. The human being, with the five senses and emotions, is alive and fully, functionally aware. This being that conducts the acts of thinking, talking, taking action, and performing daily activities is a being that has a limited existence called life.

If we could only appreciate the utter perfection and synchronicity that encompass our life-forms, we might have a better understanding of life itself. One of the primary ingredients to peace is to have more sensitivity in our lives toward others, showing less ego, more gratitude, and more kindness to strangers, and being understanding rather than judgmental toward others.

When realized, one must conquer one's insensitivity to sensitivity.

With our innate ability to reason, to take action, there is no issue too big or small that we are unable to rectify with some sort of action. Human beings seem to have a lack of passion or concern to alleviate suffering throughout the planet. We most often seem to decide that the concern is another person's or another group's responsibility. Most people do not want to take the time to contribute to assisting others. I believe that we maintain this position because of our fear of involvement, and we therefore allow someone else to become implicated in the situation, whatever it is. Perhaps we do this because of the potential consequences getting involved might bring for us.

Of course, there are precarious situations that we should avoid. Then there are situations that are not necessarily dangerous, in which our involvement would be beneficial for someone. These situations may involve providing financial help or moral support, helping a stranger, or giving general advice to someone. As Dietrich Bonhoeffer said, "Not to act is to act."

Whether people refuse to act because of possible consequences or because much of the population of the world is, unfortunately, not spiritually inclined, most people simply do not want to involve themselves in situations that may benefit strangers. Yet do we not have the power and ability to provide at least some relief of suffering within our local areas? If all of us on the planet made some sort of minuscule contribution to someone or something, would it make a difference? Of course, in this day and age, this kind of contribution may not be realistic and likely will not even be probable on a large scale in relation to the macrocosm of the planet. But our own determination and free will are important as we make our own exertions and do not wait for others to do so. In addition, it is of central importance for us to make a significant effort to perpetuate the transformation of ourselves, including our spirituality, to a higher level for at the very least our own peace.

We must have the inspiration to maintain open, self-observed minds in order to enable our receipt of higher knowledge and to sanction action for change. If there are enough humans with the awareness of goodness and the will for change, implementation is then perhaps more likely. (Kinesiology, see Section, 7 Energy) a muscle testing technique for determining truth, states that 3 percent of the world's population that generates enough positive energy can facilitate a paradigm shift in awareness or consciousness on the planet. If that were to happen, we would then be on the path to constructing a collective distinction for the good of all humankind. I believe that this new awareness or paradigm shift is already taking place. We are moving toward an individual, unique philosophy rather than submitting to the collective ideology of the current sociological perspectives. This individual philosophy is a state of mind wherein we are responsive to events from a new standpoint of understanding the self, as well as spirituality and its evolution, including religious conviction—but going beyond it.

This evolution of consciousness would also include a significant awareness of many aspects of life. How often do we appreciate the clouds, the trees, all the various types of animals, and nature itself? Think of all the perfection that currently exists on the planet. In the true reality, nothing actually causes anything else; everything is already in a self-existent, exquisite perfection of its own essence.

When was the last time we stared at a cloud, watched a sunrise, or truly appreciated a sunset? Or the last time we focused on stars in the heavens on a clear night? When have we observed a tree, its top swaying back and forth with the wind? When have we wondered at the symmetry of the trunk, the branches, and all the flawless leaves? Can we recall when we thought about the perfection of vegetables and fruit or observed the marvel of something as simple as an orange or a tomato? Vegetables and fruit have their own symmetry, their own seeds of growth or life and of their implicit replication. However, every person is the same in one sense, and yet simultaneously diverse in characteristics physically and mentally in another. We humans often take so much for granted. If we ever bring the appreciation of nature to fruition, perhaps then we will reach a higher degree of integrity and compassion, facilitated through self-elevated awareness.

Being alone to observe nature allows one a greater admiration of that which is so important for us to understand and appreciate. Nature is what maintains richness and is that which can never be lost. We assume so much; nature is so unbelievably extraordinary, and while it is always there, we may never see it.

I recall, when I had my sailing charter business, how much I appreciated being offshore for days or weeks at a time. I experienced true solitude and a stronger sense of peace, being out of sight of land, when all I could see for three hundred and sixty degrees was water and sky. There was no real connection to life onshore or to society, except a nebulous memory. I believe these isolated times enabled me to experience more significance as an individual compared to the rest of the population of the planet and to feel closer to God as universe and to nature itself.

I felt an overwhelming joy and this strong sense of peace, calm, and aliveness when I was offshore. It felt so good to be alive; I did not want to stop feeling this way.

Yet after a while, I was longing for shore and for the lifestyle that accompanies it. How much, then, did I appreciate a real shower, a stove, a real phone, and the things we have onshore and take so much for granted! It is not until one is without something that is used on a regular basis that one feels so much appreciation for that thing. However, what I cherished most of all was having my feet on land. We rarely give thought to and value the simple things in our lives.

God as universe:

Is referenced this way to denote they are one

An illustration of how we appreciate things if we don't have them for a while occurred recently in our home. We had a kitchen faucet that was making a hammering sound, and a lack of pressure resulted in just a very small stream of water. I could have called a plumber, but I kept telling my wife that I would fix the problem. Needless to say, several months went by, and the faucet remained in the same condition. The hammering stopped, but the stream grew even weaker. So I finally decided to take on the job of fixing the faucet, and I turned the water off below the sink. Then I started to disassemble and remove the faucet. Once I removed it, I could not see a problem. I replaced the center portion, and after I turned the water back on, I had no water whatsoever from the hot or cold. I left for Home Depot to buy a new faucet assembly. When I returned home, I called a plumber and explained my problem. The problem was the cartridge for the spray nozzle, and once it was removed, the water flowed strongly. I was able to correct the problem myself, with the help and direction of the plumber on the phone. I returned the faucet assembly, and I saved a service call, too.

I cannot tell you how much my wife and I appreciated what now seemed to be an extraordinary pressure and flow of water, but which in reality was normal. I found that we were saying to each other how peculiar it was to be so overwhelmed about water pressure from the kitchen sink, but we were ecstatic. I suspect our gladness came from several months of having lived with the hammering sound and with the trickle of water that I permitted to continue. When repaired, the water flow was so different, as though it were better than new, and that made us so happy. I suspect that we as humans, until we are without something in our lives that we are accustomed to, we take it for granted on a daily basis. My wife and I had never thought we could so appreciate something as simple as a kitchen faucet as much as we did then.

Unlike the kitchen faucet and understanding that problem, perhaps if we had a more comprehensive understanding and awareness of the physical world, we would gain more peace in our lives. This understanding is truly important to the planet and to our lives, even more important than money and power.

Why did I care? Why was I so concerned about what significance this had for me? I suspect that I was seeking an answer that would allow me somehow to justify and understand my own existence, which is the exploration undertaken by existentialism. But despite how important this question was to me, it did not appear to be important to others. Or perhaps they just did not talk about it—in the same way that I did not talk about it.

For some time, I struggled not to go there, to the existentialist question, but invariably I would return. I continued to struggle with a developing phobia that could hinder my ability to proceed. Yet I simply felt I needed to have a better understanding of whether there was a purpose to life and existence. I finally began to adopt a more peaceful, fearless, and less intellectual approach to the subject. This change in attitude reduced stress and resulted in a more productive understanding, allowing me to be more daring in my quest for a specific purpose to life and our existence.

About twenty-five or thirty years ago, in the course of a discussion about spirituality, a friend asked if I had the desire and will to ask God to enter my heart, soul, and mind. At first, for some reason, the idea seemed a bit frightening. I pondered the thought, and I can't recall if I repeated the request to God at that time. I thought about the phrase *enter my heart, my soul, and my mind* a great deal that day, off and on. I am not certain why I hesitated, but I spoke the phrase that night before bed and have done so every night thereafter. The phrase is currently included in my evening meditation. *Enter my heart, my soul, and my mind*—how intensely profound! I felt it to be a declaration of total, pure acceptance of God into my life.

I later added a phrase from another well-known prayer, immediately following the reciting of "enter my heart, soul, and mind," and that was "and lead me down the path of righteousness for thy name's sake." I believe that saying these prayers with focus and conviction is at least one means of displaying a true acceptance of God, and doing so has made a significant difference in my life. I know it has brought me closer to God, which has ultimately perpetuated an intimacy with the eternal.

Environmental conditioning can play a significant role in determining one's ability to maintain a quality of positive thought. A greater degree of faith, hope, and trust in God will offset to a significant degree the negativity and doubt that may have been inadvertently instilled in us in the early stages of life. Whatever it is that we are troubled with and are unable to rectify is what we should turn over to God with our declarations. We must relinquish and put into God's hands that which plagues us and that which we are unable to change, whatever it might be We must stop thinking about whatever has been difficult for us, especially if thinking about it is not going to make a positive change but will only serve to upset us even more. Turn it over to God and simply say, "I turn this issue over to you, oh Lord." Make a focused resolution, turn whatever it is over to God to rectify, and then stop thinking about it. It works for others and for me.

Chapter 3

Life and Associations

The sometimes unsolicited environmental indoctrination some of us may have been subjected to in dysfunctional households obscures our ability to realize and understand traditional values and sometimes even to function in a productive, positive manner. To overcome this problem, we would need to become aware of any negative childhood indoctrination, recognizing and rectifying any pessimistic propaganda or programming. We then could understand and implement real, true values in our life, which will ultimately perpetuate significant peace and happiness.

What are the tribulations that perpetuate dysfunction that may create inhibitions for us?

Is there anything we do not like about ourselves? What are our personalities like? Do we have a temper? Are we judgmental, sensitive, compassionate, selfish, jealous, or greedy? Do we envy others, or do we even care? Do people like us because of the power we have? Would they like us without the power? Do we agree with others simply for their acceptance? Are we reluctant at times to speak the truth? Can we facilitate an objective evaluation about ourselves and deduce whether any of these characteristics relate to us and to what extent? If we cannot, do we know who can? Could any of the characteristics mentioned earlier have been precipitated by our childhoods or environment? If we could reduce or eliminate the intensity of the negatives, might we feel better about ourselves? Could these negatives play a role in obstructing our inner peace?

Sometimes it seems that if we had more of this or more of that, we would find happiness and peace, but we will not. We must first understand that money can buy material comforts and perhaps power but that it cannot buy peace. We can achieve peace through understanding ourselves. I am not saying that if you have lots of money, you cannot be happy and have a certain amount peace; I suspect some wealthy people can. There are even those without wealth who are not happy with their lives and some that are.

I am saying that money and power are not always the answers to peace and happiness. I personally would rather have money than not. But you may attain money, power, and pleasure but not necessarily have peace. I know you have heard of people with wealth—even great wealth—that are not happy with themselves and their lives. Things that are purchased can enable instant but hollow gratification, which will ultimately diminish with time. It may appear that if we have more money or more of this or that, we will be happy. If we continue not to be happy, we may believe we simply need more. We may continue to pursue more material in search of peace and happiness, perhaps never realizing the futility in achieving more is based on only material recognition. There are services and material things we may purchase for a price, such as homes, planes, cars, boats, sex, companionship, laughter, and whatever. The exceptions are love, peace, and joy. These three things are not for sale for any dollar amount.

The achievement of happiness may be difficult. Why is it so complicated to understand what the ingredients are for obtaining *true* happiness?

The ego can dramatically inhibit personal growth in individuals. The ego tells us that subjective spiritual events are not possible. The ego tells us that the claims of religion and other belief systems are not possible without proof. The ego tells us that we must have more to be happy. It creates doubt and truly inhibits our development, spiritual and otherwise. And the destructiveness of selfishness, jealousy, envy, greed, the fear of losing our material things, and fear itself can dramatically inhibit our ability to find peace and, ultimately, happiness. But unfortunately, we are not always aware of the infection of these negative, destructive emotional forces and the slow poison they generate. We are not always aware of how others may perceive us—not to mention the way we may perceive ourselves.

These adverse emotions produce negative energy that inhibits one's ability to perceive and discern in a fruitful, positive way during the search for happiness and peace. The negative emotions or forces can corrupt decisions and produce fear. They can inhibit one's ability to evolve to a more positive place in life. It is a false belief that a given situation is stressful; rather, that is only one's perception of a situation. Have you ever wondered why your coworker or friend was upset about something that you knew would not come close to being a concern for you? One person may think a specific situation is stressful while another may not; therefore, stress comes not from the situation but from the perception of it. In other words, it is not what we see but rather how we see it. Perception and attitude play a key role in our pursuit of happiness. How we may perceive situations and the attitude we maintain is paramount to our discovery of true peace and happiness.

The strength of the negative energy from the emotions mentioned earlier determines the degree of negativity produced in the individual. One's perception, attitude, moral beliefs, environment, empirical knowledge, and emotions determine how he or she functions in life. The initial environment in one's youth—as well as other human associations—can be significant factors. However, there is also a certain degree of consciousness that is, in essence, a distinctive fingerprint of each human soul. I believe that an innate presence determines the purity of the integrity, morality, or higher levels of consciousness in all of us. For example, notice the difference between historical figures such as Mao Zedong, Joseph Stalin, and Adolf Hitler, compared with, say, Jesus, Moses, or Muhammad.

The disparity of these individuals is enormous. Some would certainly be the antitheses of others. Is such a monumental difference simply accidental, or is there some sort of basis in the hypothesis that there is some innate characteristic in each of these people? The inconsistency between different levels of consciousness does exist, and there does not seem to be a better explanation for the dichotomy in the actions of individuals.

I firmly believe that there are innate degrees of consciousness among individuals, which vary from person to person and are determined before birth, in the later period of the third trimester. I will discuss the basis of this belief and process later. But I believe I can state without reservation that individuals are born with distinctively different physical and mental characteristics and different degrees of consciousness, in the same way that we all have different fingerprints. There is some logic behind this idea; for example, kinesiology is a muscle-testing technique that is thought to validate truth and indicates that there are different degrees of consciousness in individuals. I will discuss this further in the chapter on energy.

While I believe that the consciousness difference in mental characteristics manifests in the embryonic stages, I also believe that just as we enter this world with different fingerprints, so do we with distinct differences in levels of consciousness. The elevation of the baseline of consciousness or awareness of a given individual may be escalated through meditation or spirituality, through events that occur in life, and through the person having an open, self-observing mind. In addition, as the person ages, he or she may reach a certain degree of wisdom through his or her own sensitivity. When an individual has a lower degree of integrity or a lack of integrity, he or she may also present difficulties in improving the baseline of consciousness. Without the ability to recognize a problem or the desire for improvement, the result, on a smaller scale, may be a level of criminality, and on a larger scale, may be a complete radicalization and a totalitarianism attitude.

With low levels of integrity, such people may not realize that the way in which they conduct themselves is inconsistent with appropriate behavior in our society—or they may realize that their behavior is inappropriate and simply not care. In either instance, the low level of integrity or the lack thereof may present extreme issues for the individuals and for those surrounding them.

Chapter 4

Realization of Purpose

In ancient China, the keeper of the Imperial Library, Lao Tzu, was famous for his wisdom. The treatise he is thought to have written, the *Tao Te Ching* "The Way of Life, or Integrity," is one of the most influential books in history and is one of the most famous books of Chinese spirituality. Written over twenty-five hundred years ago, it is a book of philosophy for individuals.

In this treatise, one of the most profound questions and answers is a student asks his teacher, "Master, what is real?" and the master replies, "That which is real never changes."

In our reality, that which is real, only the immortal soul does not change or die. However, in the same reality, everything other than the soul can change or may ultimately cease to exist. Everything changes: nature, humanity, animals, vegetation, everything living and nonliving. The sun, moon, stars, planets, mountains, rivers, landmasses, buildings, and other structures will all eventually change or, over hundreds or thousands of years cease to exist. The only permanence in life and existence is impermanence.

Regarding aspects of life that change, I believe we first must understand that there are no accidents in the universe. Everything in the universe is in a state of perfection. Even with everything's natural evolutionary changes or ultimate demise, everything maintains a synchronicity (orchestrated), a consistent perfection that manifests according to the design of the Divine. All that is, simply is orchestrated to its own purpose, identification, and perfection during its existence.

Optimum fulfillment in life emanates from finding one's daily purpose and functioning according to that purpose. This ultimately will perpetuate peace, and it will eventually manifest joy, the by-product of peace. *Joy* and *peace* supply a good degree of happiness. When coupled with the fortune of *romantic love*, they are the *epitome* or the ultimate form of true happiness on the planet.

The kinds of purpose I refer to might be those things that give one's daily job or work a greater degree of significance—work that one receives compensation for that does not seem like work, but rather, seems like joyful pleasure, a work where passion exists. We often find ourselves in positions or professions that we don't like or that just seem mediocre. If we could select our way of life and our work, knowing we could not fail regardless what they were, what would we choose? What does that inner voice from your heart say? What does the voice from within say that calls us to express ourselves? I know that I knew the answer to that question; I did not have to ask myself. My own answer is oil painting, for which I have the most insatiable desire and in which I find the utmost pleasure.

When I walk into my studio and start painting, with classical music—or my very favorite, Puccini arias—playing in the background, I am transported somewhere else. I am truly living in the moment. Time even has a way of quickly slipping by; hours almost seem like minutes. Time seems timeless when I am painting. I seem so true to my purpose, God's gift to me that I have never truly concentrated on to its fullest. If only I had followed my heart in the beginning, many years ago, that inner voice from within that said to me, stay with painting!

I recall returning from Florida and meeting with my cousin, Barry, for lunch at a quaint little restaurant in south St. Louis called the Sidney Street Café. It rather reminded me of a European café. We sat at a table for two, and my back was to the wall. We began having a conversation about what I would like to do with my life now that I had returned from Florida. I distinctly remember saying to Barry, "I just don't know what I want to do with my life." Within seconds of that statement, an oil painting fell off the wall, onto my head and shoulder. The painting was about eighteen by twenty-four inches with the frame. I was more stunned than hurt, slightly bruised on my head, but nothing more.

The mere fact that there was no disturbance of any kind—weather, thunder, and earthquake—was remarkable. Afterward, I thought to myself, here I make a statement that I do not know what I want to do with my life, and what happens? An oil painting falls off the wall. Is this not God's way of telling me this is what I should be doing? Is this not God saying, "What do I have to do, hit you in the head with a painting for you to realize this is what you need to do with your life?" Yet, I still did not heed this event, what I would call divine intervention. But I paint more often now, in addition to my regular work. What I have learned from my experiences is that the fear of failure can be significant if one permits it to be so. This reminds me of the old expression, "If I knew then what I know today, how different life might be."

Is that not why we read and study, to learn from history or perhaps from others mistakes and to keep from repeating our own? How many times do we make the same mistake? Why can we not appreciate and utilize the empirical knowledge we gain from mistakes? When will we pass life's course instead of repeatedly having to relearn? How many times must we make the same mistakes and take the same course over, the different lessons of life? "I should never have done this, or I should of never have done that. I cannot believe I did that again." How many times do we have to make the same mistake before we finally learn?

I recall a story from my own history that illustrates this tendency to make the same mistakes multiple times. I was sailing on the west coast of Florida and heading into a channel of a populated area. At this point, I suddenly felt the boat come to an abrupt halt, and I realized I had gone aground. It was extremely difficult to pull the boat out; in fact, being towed was the only way out of the situation.

The next day, I was sailing down the same channel, but this time, I stayed more to the center. But I went aground again. It was extremely difficult to motor out, and it took about three hours and a higher tide to accomplish it. A couple of days later, I was sailing down the same channel, and this time I was approaching the channel at a much higher tide. But I could not believe that, for whatever reason, I was aground again. After about two hours or so, I was able to motor out, much more quickly this time.

The next time I was in the area, the chart indicated that the depth was okay, and the tide was even higher. But it was not okay, and I went aground once again. The next time I was in the same area, I decided to take another channel.

As for my own mistakes, I can only try to learn from them. I can only attempt to understand when enough is enough and when to change course and take another direction or path to pursue what I am looking for or trying to achieve. I can only try to develop the ability to know which bridges to burn and which not to burn.

I love to paint in oil. I have had one-man shows, which is a one-person art exhibit but I am never completely satisfied with my work. I still feel to this day that I have not attained the degree of expression I desire in my work. I suppose the reason that I have not jumped into full-time painting is that, at least in the beginning, I could not have met my financial obligations. When I was younger, without financial or other obligations, perhaps then it would have been more suitable to become a full-time artist. One could wonder, if this was my true passion, why I didn't pursue it then.

One reason was that I permitted friends, family, and others whom I admired in the business world to influence me. The respected path for me to follow was business to gain great wealth. But we need to acquire the recognition and understanding of our heart's desire to be our own person and to follow it. One should not permit his or her life path to be influenced by the expectations of others.

Puccini's opera *La Bohème* is about three men living together in an apartment. One is an artist, one a poet, and the third a writer. Financially broke but psychologically rich, they are doing what they love. They express this in one portion of the opera in which they sing, "We are so happy in our poverty." Think about that statement: *We are so happy in our poverty.* Now, that may be construed as an ultimate form of commitment, fervor, and dedication for one's work. They are doing what their hearts desire, truly savoring their passion, with material things being secondary. All they care about is their work.

How much passion and fervor do we have for that which we love and desire? What are we willing to sacrifice to achieve our heart's desire and passion? Once achieved, the performing of our heart's desire would facilitate joy and an aliveness and fulfillment in our lives that we may never have experienced before.

31

My father and mother had mediocre lives, but were content with where they were. So I think my business desires were instilled by my brother-in-law, Lester. He is truly a self-made, wealthy man. When he married my sister, he was virtually penniless, but he built a huge corporation worth several hundred million dollars. However, business was not my true passion. I was in denial about what was truly important to me.

If we could only listen to the voice from our heart, the gut feeling prompting us to do what would give us great pleasure and satisfaction! But for whatever reason, we do not listen. I believe that we fear our inability to accomplish our desires, or we fear failure or whatever else may cast a negative shadow on our life's goals. Perhaps friends or relatives cast the shadows and enable the fear of failure to surface. But our daily work, our livelihood, should be that which gives us significant pleasure. Our work should not be just a job we really do not like, or that is just okay or that is only comfortable.

The movie *The International* has a line that depicts an interesting scenario: "Sometimes a man's destiny may be met on a road he took to avoid it." At the time I heard this, I felt that it was very profound. It had such depth for me that I thought about it a great deal. This quote actually derived from the writings of the French writer Jean de La Fontaine:

"A person often meets his destiny on the road he took to avoid it."

Ironically, as the quotation describes, I now find myself today writing the thoughts and words about that which I sought to avoid over forty years ago: existentialism.

Perhaps there is a destiny for some of us, or all of us, that we ultimately meet on the road we took either to avoid it or to avoid what we feared. As a result, we comprise pursuing our heart's desire for much of our lives.

When our heart's desire is recognized, the answer is that if, at this time in our lives, we are unable to accomplish our desire on a full-time basis, we might capture it on a part-time basis for now. We should seek out that which we would like to accomplish part-time and not stop until we find it and then do it!

If you do not know what it is that may be your passion, then ask yourself, "What would I do as my life's work if I knew I could not be unsuccessful?" Alternatively, perhaps, "What would I choose if I knew I could not fail?" What would it be?

There was a time in my life when I felt that sailing was my interest. I spent many years on the Mississippi River, learning to sail and then taking a long jaunt down the Mississippi, from St. Louis to New Orleans and ultimately to the Gulf of Mexico. I spent nearly six years in Florida as a United States Coast Guard licensed Captain. I also started a sailing charter boat business. The sailing life was a lifestyle of much adventure, I must say. I was in my mid-forties, and at this time in my life, I lived my dream. At one time, I owned a thirty-eight-foot Endeavour Aft Cockpit Sloop and a seventy-two-foot gaff-rigged schooner. The Schooner was all steel but built to resemble a mid nineteenth–century trading ship. She had three staterooms, two heads and showers, a galley, a nice-size navigation station, and a huge grand salon. She was licensed for forty-nine passengers.

Although I loved the lifestyle of adventure and spent almost six years on the west coast of Florida in the sailing charter business, the business was not generating enough income to maintain itself. I left the Florida charter business and lifestyle to return to St. Louis in 1992.

After returning to St. Louis, I dated a woman for a short period that knew I had an interest in spiritual healing and meditation. About six months after we stopped seeing each other, I received a phone call from a woman who had obtained my phone number from the lady I had dated. She asked if I was interested in "healing through energy." I said

33

that at this time, I was not, because I was involved in "meditating and manifesting." However, I added, "If you would leave the phone number of the place mentioned, perhaps later I might be interested." The last four digits of the phone number were 8557. My childhood address when I lived with my parents was also 8557. The odds against seeing this exact same permutation of numbers were extraordinary. I felt that the phone number was significant and much more than a coincidence, if you even believe in coincidence. So I later contacted the healing center in St. Louis for information about classes and courses. The name of the energy-healing group was Spiritual Human Yoga (SHY). The group has recently undergone a name change to Mankind Enlightenment Love (MEL).

This MEL group teaches the practice of healing through Universal Energy (UE), which is similar but different in what some cultures call *Prana, Chi,* or *Ki,* learning the technique for transferring healing energy from one body to another. UE is an ancient method based on the concept that our bodies, when attuned to channel and use UE for healing, using the body's chakra system as a conduit. Chakras are one of seven spiritual centers in the body according to Sanskrit and yoga philosophy. Anyone, regardless of educational or spiritual background, can learn to channel this energy to enhance the body's natural ability to heal. I will elaborate on this in more detail in the chapter on Energy.

For thousands of years, philosophers have come to at least one understanding: that there is only one material, and that we therefore are all interconnected. This connection is identified as consciousness, awareness, spirit, nirvana, or God. It is continuous, ever present, and unalterable, and it is the essence of all that is.

SECTION 2

Spirituality

Chapter 5

Belief Systems

Do we believe that the lord's creation occurred in the seven days as described in the first chapter of Genesis? Up until recently, science theorized that there was no beginning to the universe, a theory that contradicted the account in Genesis. Now, with the theory of the big bang, does that confirm that the events in Genesis occurred as they were written? Could this be possible? If the universe was born with the big bang, is all of space now the universe? If there was no universe before the big bang, what existed? Was it simply a void, an empty space devoid of planets, stars, fundamental particles, and atoms? If nothing existed before the universe, is all of space now considered to be the universe and all that is infinite? Alternatively, is there a space not considered part of the universe?

If there was nothing before, and now the universe exists through the big bang or creation, was what existed before the big bang simply nothing? Moreover, what is nothing—a place where not anything exists? Simply using the process of elimination and deduction, an area that consists of no space, nothing, a void, is still an area, a space where nothing is, nothing still remains as something. The something is an area where there is not anything, as we know it—no material substance, but simply emptiness in space. The empty void in space remains credible as something, even though nothing as we know of exists of there. The space remains an area where something unknown exists. This space may encompass an unknown area of identification. Logic, deduction, and whether science had a means for determination would dictate that something must exist beyond the end of something else. The existence of the unknown void itself is something. Some people would say that there must be an end to the universe; if so, what is beyond the end? Is it more space or is it nothing? If more space, then the universe has not ended. If nothing, then it still has not ended, because nothing is something. Nothing is something, and end denotes the finality of what? Is the end a wall, a fence, a partition, a body of water, or a sign that says end of the universe—what kind of end? We have the end of a street, the end of your home, the end of your car, the end of the field, the end of this, and the end of that, but there is always something beyond the end of whatever it is.

The purpose of this comparison is to show that something did exist before the big bang, even though it was considered emptiness or nothing. If nothing else, God as universe existed before the big bang, inasmuch as God is without a beginning and without an end.

Was there something before God existed? Was God always there? Was God indeed without a beginning and without an end? Can we comprehend infinity? Can we comprehend a supreme being without a beginning and without end? If God always was, is, and shall be, can we realize this paradigm? Can we understand infinity and a forever God? A forever-supreme force that always was, is, and always shall be?

Spirituality is described in many ways, some of which include a belief in a superior, intelligent presence that exists in the universe and which is significantly greater than humans and which maintains a connection with all that is living. In addition, spirituality describes a realization and an awareness of the true purpose and meaning of life and the improvement and expansion of essential personal and spiritual values. Spirituality is a practice where one finds meaning, hope, faith, comfort, and peace in one's life. Spirituality is often connected with religion; however, it does not need to be unless one desires it to be so.

Many people find an equal or greater reward in spirituality as a belief in itself, as a religion, or as a mix with a religion. A Christian may define spirituality as the purity of his or her relationship with Christ. A Buddhist, a Muslim, or a Jew would have different definitions of spirituality altogether. Atheists and agnostics could be considered a form of spirituality within themselves. Spirituality in itself may mean to some simply having a belief in a superior intelligence throughout the universe, without necessarily adding a religious affiliation. Spirituality could also include an awareness and understanding of oneself, as well as a realization of positive values and or a relationship to nature. Spirituality and religion can be a belief system in and of itself that may ultimately control our behavior. A belief system can be a belief in anything and is usually instilled in us in the early stages of life by our religion and by our parents and other individuals, all of which influence us to a significant degree.

There are approximately forty organized religions in the world. The following are some of the top religions in terms of numbers of adherents. Several of the following I indicate to be collections of similar religions in different groups.

39

1) Christianity: 2.1 billion

2) Islam: 1.5 billion

3) Hinduism: 900 million

4) Chinese traditional collection of many religions: 394 million

5) Buddhism: 376 million

6) Primal indigenous, collection of smaller religions: 300 million

7) African traditional diasporic, collection of smaller religions of African origin: 100 million

8) Sikhism: 23 million

9) Spiritism, general approach to an idea of spirits: 15 million

10) Judaism: 14 million

If we could only go beyond our belief systems and realize that God, life, meaning, and purpose are subjects that we could actually know about rather than assume. Your belief systems, or religion, may be reinforced with a new awareness by the time you finish this section or the book.

Prayers can be a significant part of religious belief systems and of spirituality. One of the most inspirational prayers, to me, is the Peace Prayer of Saint Francis of Assisi. The prayer first appeared in the French magazine *La Clochette* around 1912, and it does not appear in any known writings of Saint Francis himself. The prayer is suspected to have been written by Father Bouquerel, but this was never confirmed. It was referred to as the Prayer of Saint Francis because it was often seen on a small card with the picture of the saint on one side and the prayer on the other side.

Saint Francis was born in about 1182. After a carefree youth, he turned his back on family and wealth and committed himself to God. He lived simple—a life of poverty. He established the rule of Saint

Francis, which exists today as the Order of Saint Francis, referred to as the Franciscans. He died in 1226 at the age of forty-four. The peace prayer, because it is nonsectarian in context, can be applied to any religion or spiritual practice. It can even be used in a non-spiritual way or if one has no religious belief system at all.

***

The Peace Prayer of Saint Francis
O Lord, make me an instrument of Thy Peace!
Where there is hatred, let me sow love.
Where there is injury, pardon.
Where there is doubt, faith.
Where there is despair, hope.
Where there is darkness, light.
Where there is sadness, joy.
Oh Divine Master, grant that I may not
so much seek to be consoled as to console;
to be understood as to understand;
to be loved as to love; for it is in giving that we receive; it is in
pardoning that we are pardoned; and it is in dying that we are born
to Eternal Life.
Amen

***

Could any other writing have such depth of purpose and truth or direct one to righteousness with such simplicity and within such a short span of words? The prayer truly depicts love, sensitivity, compassion, understanding, and a positive attitude. Would it be difficult for people to follow the basic philosophy of the prayer in their lives? I think not! If only more people could live their lives based on the principles of the prayer, regardless of religion, culture or belief, how different a world it would be!

In the course of my daily mediation, I include the prayer of Saint Francis before each session, sometimes saying it aloud. When I do this, there are instances when I become emotional, with tears streaming down my face. Despite being stated with such simplicity, there is just something profound that makes the prayer so inspirational and so powerful.

Without empirical knowledge regarding religion, spirituality, or anything else in life, it is essential that we understand the importance of a belief system and realize how important it is to have and maintain one in our lives. A person's belief system pertaining to religion or society is the set of beliefs he or she has and maintains about what is right and wrong, what is true and false, and what is proper or not.

Beliefs we may maintain about religion, spirituality, or our perceptions of virtually anything usually come without verifiable proof, evidence, or experience. Beliefs influence our behaviors and preclude the requirement of facts. On what do we base our beliefs, regarding anything? What someone else has said? What someone said someone else has said or done? What is the basis of our beliefs? How important to us is the basis we maintain for believing? Are our beliefs based on or influenced by our actual desires? Would we feel more comfortable if we had more support for what we believe, other than what other people have stated and what we have read from texts, even though they are very well respected by society?

I do not mean to insinuate that belief systems are not important—quite the contrary. The belief system dictates a belief in an event or in something or someone; it influences our perception of what we see. Some beliefs stem from alleged facts conveyed to others from perhaps hundreds or even thousands of years ago. We might believe in those who are usually respected and recognized by others for their opinions and contributions and sometimes their education. Their stature enables us to accept that which they believe and wish to convey to us.

Other reasons for acceptance of a belief system might stem from fear or virtually anything of concern. Most of us need belief systems to help alleviate the fear of death or of the unknown. In addition, we may adopt a belief system to explain what we cannot understand or define, for our own peace of mind. We may adopt belief systems for our work, home, spouse, friends, or other things we need to believe in. I suppose we all have some sort of belief system. Even having no belief is a belief system; having no belief system is in fact then one's "belief system." Non-belief in any religion or God is one's belief that no God or religion is worthy of belief; that would be a belief system. My belief is in a superior intelligence, God, as universe. My belief system most recently has been blessed with more of an actual knowing through personal experiences.

I am certain we have all heard the expression, "I will put the fear of God in you." Should we actually fear God? Is there some necessity and purpose in fearing God? Should we fear God to preclude any wrongful deeds we may commit? Do we believe we should fear God because we should be afraid not to? Do we ever express how we feel about God? Do we live our lives righteously in fear of the wrath of God, or do we live our life righteously because that is who we are?

I think the following quotation is important to learn or to reaffirm. Pierre Teilhard de Chardin was a French Jesuit priest who lived in the late nineteenth and early twentieth centuries. He was trained as both a paleontologist and a philosopher. He is famous for saying, "We are not human beings having a spiritual experience; we are spiritual beings having a human experience."

Is our religion important as a belief system? Do we not need religion and our God to reinforce the idea that when we cease to exist, it is not complete darkness forever, but that there is a life after death? What a horrific thought it would be that when we die, it is blackness or nothingness forever! However, if you do not fear blackness or nothingness and believe you will not be aware of anything, you may just be fine with that belief.

There are those who have the good fortune of gaining empirical knowledge through spiritual events. When this happens, their belief in an afterlife is no longer simply a belief but can be considered an actual, factual knowing that there is a form of existence after the spirit leaves the physical body. I will return to this idea later.

Summary of Belief Systems

1)   It is essential that we understand the importance of having and maintaining a belief system in our lives.

2)   Beliefs we may maintain about religion, spirituality, and our perception of virtually anything are usually without verifiable poof, evidence, or experience.

3)   Belief influences our behavior and precludes the requirement of facts.

4)   What is the basis of our beliefs? Are our beliefs based on or influenced by our actual desires?

5)   We often believe someone who is usually respected and recognized by others for his or her opinions, contributions, and sometimes his or her education. The person's stature enables us to accept that which he or she believes and wishes to convey to us.

6)   Most of us need a belief system to help fill the gap we may maintain regarding fear.

7)   Even having no belief is thought by some to be a belief system in itself.

8)   Grief and mourning are important for healing and for limiting anxiety experienced by the individual for any loss.

9)   How we perceive a given situation is critical for our acceptance.

10) Understanding that we must live in the present moment and not permit any negative aspect of the past to surface is paramount.

11) Do we live our lives righteously because that is who we are?

For the moment, forget about what philosophers and some psychologists sometimes teach from a subjective platform about the subject of existence. Let us actually be logical about what we know and what we have experienced in addition to belief systems. How much proof do we need to know the truth about God? Do we not know that evidence is the basis for law of any sort, including physics or government? We know that our knowledge, truth, and experiences support our lives. Is life, then, not an actual knowing, based on factual truths or tangible evidence, something that is visually seen and touchable? We believe in what we can see, touch, smell, hear, and taste.

Assume one is in a jungle or a rainforest, walking with no visible life or material objects of any kind around to be seen. In addition, for the sake of this illustration, let's say the person knows of no other life forms, no society, or human-made material objects. Let's call this person the observer. He or she has been walking for hours, and nothing is visible but the normal earth or vegetation. Suddenly, after many hours of walking, the person finds a wristwatch. The observer does not know what it is, and he or she has never seen anything like it. You and I would know that it is a name-brand chronograph made of stainless steel and having a colored dial of black-and-white mother-of-pearl with Roman numerals on the face. It has the day, the date, a stopwatch, and a second hand. The bracelet is also of stainless steel. The object has uniformity and symmetry, it is hard to the touch, it shines, and it makes a ticking sound. It looks like nothing the observer has ever seen before. The observer picks up this strange object and examines it. If you were the observer, what would you think of the find? What would your first thought be? How would you react?

Would you think that the watch was just another part of the rainforest? Likely not, as it is too different from the normal surroundings.

The observer thinks, *what is this? How did it get here? Where did it come from?* Does he or she think it simply evolved? The person remembers walking this way before without ever noticing it. Did it simply just appear? Perhaps it was uncovered after being buried by a mudslide. But he or she finally decides that the object is too dramatically different from anything he or she has ever seen.

The observer believes this is too unbelievable an object just to have grown or evolved; he or she cannot explain it. He or she may think that someone or something must have created the object, because this thing is just too different compared to anything else the observer has ever seen and too beautiful and complex to have simply evolved on its own. The person looks around for another person or something that could have created or caused this object to exist. The, observer is frightened and keeps throwing glances over their shoulder, thinking that perhaps he or she is not alone. The person does not understand what to believe. Should the observer even care how the object appeared? Is the person curious? He or she would like to find an answer, knowing that it is not possible simply to believe the object just appeared. Nevertheless, if it did just appear, what caused it to do so? Something had to have caused or created this intricate, complex, and beautiful object.

Why is it so difficult for some of us to accept that there is a superior presence in the universe? Must we hear God's voice or see God? Sometimes we may feel that if God does not answer our prayers, then God cannot exist.

Some people may say that Darwin's theory of evolution explains how life began. I would say to those people that if that is so, then evolution was God's mechanism for the creation of life. Darwin's theory never does mention very much about the origin of the origin of the species, what actually caused the existence of the organism that was the beginning of his investigation regarding evolution. Darwin, of course, never had the sophisticated equipment we maintain today for biological experiments. Do we believe that life and the planet were accidents? Or did a superior force create the earth, the universe, and humankind?

Consider the scope of all creation on the planet, and take the ocean, in its awesome beauty and power, as an example. Recall how the ocean perpetuates a wave, a crest, and the movement of the water, and see the diverse colors. Note the way in which the ocean almost has a breath, inhaling and exhaling, rising and falling in its movement, as if it is alive. Think of the different life forms the ocean maintains. Notice the different temperaments, the calm and tumultuous characteristics the ocean presents, like the vicissitudes of a person's temperament. Remember the serene and violent sides the ocean has retained for so many millions of years.

Water itself is colorless, odorless, and tasteless. Yet living entities cannot survive without water. The human body itself consists of 60 percent water. Water has a boiling point of 212 degrees Fahrenheit and a freezing point of 32 degrees Fahrenheit. Water permits our bodies to undergo environmental changes and yet maintain an average body temperature of 98.6 degrees Fahrenheit. Water is neutral as far as chemical composition, so it enables and permits vitamins, nutrients, minerals, and medicines to be absorbed and carried throughout our bodies. About 75 percent of the planet is water as well. And nature has an incredible way of using the process of evaporation to remove the water from the oceans and leave the salt, then distribute it throughout the planet to many places where it is needed.

The sky is a gorgeous blue on a clear day, and sometimes the soft, silky, exquisite clouds interweave throughout. The sky has similar characteristics to the ocean, exhibiting both calm and tumultuous activity at different times through changing weather. We see the sky with its ubiquitous blue, gray, and white that is so forever there. Sometimes we see glittering rays of sunlight permeating through clouds with an almost surreal sheen to them.

Then think of the planet perfectly suspended in space, at the exact proper distance from the sun. Any closer to the sun, and the planet would burn up. Any further away from the sun, and the planet would freeze. The earth is ninety-three million miles from the sun, and it takes light from the sun about eight minutes to reach the earth, at a speed of one hundred eighty-six thousand miles per second. The earth circles the sun at an approximate speed of sixty-seven thousand miles per hour, and at the same time, it rotates on its axis as it circles the sun. This in turn enables the surface of the earth to cool and warm evenly and properly. As far as scientists know at the moment, the earth is thus far the only known planet that has the exact correct atmospheric mixture of substances to sustain all our life forms. The atmosphere we enjoy today is dramatically different from the atmosphere that formed with the Earth billions of years ago. With time, the Earth's life-giving atmosphere formed and is what we live with today: twenty-one percent oxygen, seventy-eight percent nitrogen, and about one percent argon and carbon dioxide.

Everything on the planet currently remains in a state of consistent perfection, even when there are changes for human or other forms of life. Perfection remains as perfection in itself. When leaves turn color and fall, this is part of the trees' natural process of evolution. Humans remain in perfection even with age and body changes. Our sun with its tremendous explosions from within, including solar flares, remains in perfection in and of itself. All entities in and of themselves with changes due to time continually remain in their own perfection for the current period in their existence. Think of the sunrise and the sunset and the way the moon rises and sets or how its phases change. Think of the ocean tides, of gravity, of the twenty-four hours between sunrise and sunset, or how water can change to ice and then back to water or to a vapor. Think of all natural occurrences that exist and continually change.

Imagine the human brain and its abilities in processing so much information so rapidly—millions of messages in one second. Recall how humans have the ability to think, to reason, to sense emotions, and to experience pain, pleasure, love, hate, fear, guilt, sensitivity, concern, passion, and so on. Humans have the ability to take action, to walk, to talk, to listen, to create, and to empathize with others. Think of the perfection and abilities of other organs like the eye, heart, lungs, and all the many others.

Deoxyribonucleic acid (DNA) is the essence of life, the program code of life. It is the hereditary substance in humans and in almost all other organisms. Most DNA is located in the cell nucleus, and almost every cell in a person's body has the same DNA. The different arrangements of genes determine the way DNA controls how many fingers we have, where our legs are placed on our bodies, and the color of our eyes. It is the arrangement of the DNA in us that determines the different characteristics that each of us has.

Science has proven that the process of sequences followed each time for cell production and replication makes it virtually impossible for the DNA process to have happened accidentally. Complicated software programs developed by experienced, sophisticated minds through many months or years of effort seem like child's play compared to the DNA process. DNA is so much more complicated with the abundance and sequences of processes involved.

"Something had to create the genetic code; it did not create itself," said Dr. Gerald Schroeder, a scientist with over thirty years of experience in research and teaching. His doctorate is in two fields: earth sciences and physics. His book, *The Hidden Face of God*, provides positive reasons for faith, from the wisdom encoded in DNA and analyzed by science to the integrated complexity of cellular life.

Stephen C. Meyer has a PhD in the Philosophy of Science from Cambridge University in England and is a former geophysicist and college professor. He does have an explanation for how life on Earth began: "The DNA in every cell of every creature shows unmistakable evidence of having been deliberately designed by an intelligent being."

[Gerald L.] [Schroeder]. [*The Hidden Face of GOD*]
(Free Press, April 30 2002)
[Stephen L.] Meyer] [*Signature in the Cell*]
(Harper One, June 22, 2010)

Anthony Flew Denounces Atheism-Excerpt

LONDON, November 2, 2007 (LifeSiteNews.com) – Former Darwinian atheist philosopher Anthony Flew has published a new book, "There Is a God: How the World's Most Notorious Atheist Changed His Mind," to explain his move from being one of the world's leading exponents of the pure materialist Darwinian philosophy to belief in the existence of a personal deity who created the universe. Flew, an Oxford educated philosopher described by some as "legendary", first announced his discovery of "a god" in 2004. Flew had been one of the 20th century's leading proponents of the pure atheistic Darwinian doctrines that categorically reject any possibility of a creative divine being. His ideas paved the way for thinkers such as Richard Dawkins, the UK's most virulent opponent of religious belief.

As reported in the *New York Times,* the *Los Angeles Times,* and the *Chicago Tribune* in 2007, after reading *The Hidden Face of God* by Gerald Schroeder and *The Wonder of the World* by Roy Varghese, Antony Flew, the world's most influential atheist philosopher, abandoned his belief in a godless world. *He publicly apologized for leading so many people astray during the decades in which he maintained his atheistic platform.*

This excerpt is from the *New York Times Magazine,* November 4, 2007.

> *The startling article appeared originally on Dec. 9, 2004. "A British philosophy professor who has been a leading champion of atheism for more than a half-century has changed his mind," Richard Ostling of The Associated Press wrote. "He now believes in God— more or less—based on scientific evidence and says so on a video released Thursday. At age 81, after decades of insisting belief is a mistake, Antony Flew has concluded that some sort of intelligence or first cause must have created the universe. A super intelligence is the only good explanation for the origin of life and the complexity of nature, Flew said in a telephone interview from England."*

> *There was also mention in a November 7, 2007, New York Times Magazine article of that the aging Flew's health was declining and the declaration about the existence of God was falsely influenced by*

some of his colleagues. However, Flew, in the same article, disputed the claim and stated his decision was based strictly on science.

The following is an excerpt from an article by Gerald Schroeder:
Very occasionally, monkeys hammering away on typewriters will type out one of Shakespeare's sonnets. NOT TRUE. The laws of probability confirm that the universe would have reached its heat of death before getting one sonnet. We will never get a sonnet by random trials, and the most basic molecules of life are far more complex than the most intricate sonnet.

LifeSiteNews.com:
[Hilary] [White] *"Former Atheist Darwinian Explains his Conversion in a New Book"*
November 2, 2007

New York Times Magazine:
[Mark] [Oppenheimer] *"The Turning of an Atheist"*
November 4, 2007

Associated Press:
[Richard] [Ostling]
December 9, 2004

[Gerald L.] [Schroeder]. [*The Hidden Face of GOD]*
(Free Press, April 30 2002)

There are countless numbers of atheists that who have renounced atheism and turned to the belief in a superior intelligence that created life due to the science of DNA and the integrated complexity surrounding it. The Associated Press, Richard Ostling reported December 9, 2004, that leading atheist Antony Flew now believes in a God. David Attenborough, Naturalist Broadcaster for the BBC, said on January 30, 2012, "God may exist." On February 24, 2012, on the website Telegraph. Com., UK, Oxford Scholar Professor Richard Dawkins renounced Atheism: "I Cannot be Sure God Does Not Exist." By, John Bingham, Religious Affairs Editor. All of these belief changes are due to the science of DNA.

I feel I should share with you an incredible experience that occurred after I navigated down the Mississippi River from St. Louis, Missouri, to New Orleans, Louisiana, which was an experience in itself. In the spring, the Mississippi River has a current running at about five to six knots. At night, the river is too difficult and dangerous to navigate. If you are operating a towboat with barges, and if you have a proper knowledge of the river and the very essential lighting capabilities, then operating at night could be fine. We would stop overnight at Civil War towns like Natchez and Vicksburg, which was a real treat.

This adventure occurred upon departing the port of New Orleans. I was on a schedule to get my boat to Punta Gorda, Florida, on the west coast. A friend named Sarah accompanied me on the journey from New Orleans to Punta Gorda, a distance of approximately five hundred nautical miles. Before leaving New Orleans, we docked at a marina on Lake Ponchartrain. There just is not any place to dock on the river other than in barge staging areas. This type of facility is usually not permitted for non-workboats, and it was not very suitable, anyway.

My sailing vessel was an Endeavour sloop, thirty-eight feet in length, with a 12.6-foot beam or width and one mast. There was a forward cabin, a galley, a head, a grand salon, and a navigation station and quarter berth. The boat was constructed of fiberglass and was very well built and strong. Before leaving on an offshore trip, the prudent thing to do is to go through a safety checklist that includes but is not limited to fuel, water, oil, through hull fittings, fire equipment, and so on.

When we were satisfied that all was in order, we were ready to shove off the next day. But before departing New Orleans, I checked the weather and found that there was a good chance of heavy seas. It seems that in sailing, as sometimes in life, when you are on a schedule, there is a greater chance of potential problems. I elected to depart, thinking that the weather would not be that bad. As we were leaving the port of New Orleans and exiting through the main ship channel rather than via the Mississippi River, we noticed many fishing trawlers returning. The ship channel is a much more direct path to the Gulf of Mexico and accommodates large overseas traffic, cruise boats, tankers, and cargo ships. It is interesting to note that you could find large ships of this nature as far north on the Mississippi to Donaldsonville, Louisiana.

Our departure began to seem more questionable as we watched the fishing trawlers return to port. It seemed as though we were the only vessel going out to sea. However, we continued out the ship channel to the Gulf of Mexico. The sun had already set before we reached the gulf. It was now about 8:30 p.m., and the waves were about three to four feet. We had eaten dinner before we shoved off, so food was not necessary. We had docked at Lake Ponchartrain for several days before leaving, so we were getting our sea legs back.

It was an overcast night; there were no stars, and the thick air began to become a bit chilly. The winds picked up after about an hour to about fifteen to twenty knots. (One knot represents about .85 of a mile per hour.) I was under full sail, but reduced the sail area. The seas were beginning to build and reduction of sails would be difficult to accomplish later. We were really cooking on the point of sail called a broad reach. We were doing a speed of about six knots. The seas continued to build, and so did the wind, which was now about thirty knots, about gale force.

Usually, the stronger the wind, the less sail you will carry. The size of the boat will determine the total sail area required for any sailing vessel. The bigger the boat is, the larger the sail area, and the smaller the boat, the less the sail area. This boat was a thirty-eight-foot Endeavour aft cockpit named the *Marsha Ann 2*. I knew she was a well-built boat and could take punishment if necessary. However, I was not so sure about Sarah and myself.

It was rough. We both became seasick, which contributed to what I call "total body purification." That is when your bowels, bladder, and stomach have been completely emptied, and you feel a very unpleasant and distinctive type of nausea. It was difficult to go below to take a fix on our position because of how rough the seas were. To go below, you really needed a football helmet and shoulder pads. So I was not taking the hourly position fix that I knew I should be taking, which would have been the prudent thing to do.

I do not know any other way to explain what happened except that gradually, the seas continued to build, and for whatever reason, the wind began to diminish. The seas became larger and larger and at times seemed confused. Eventually, the seas became so large that I had to drop all sail and turn on the diesel engine. Unbelievably, some of the seas were almost blanketing the sails. The top of the main mast was fifty-eight feet off the water. Gradually, we began to climb these huge waves. The experience reminded me of the slow climb you experience on a rollercoaster ride at an amusement park, rolling up with the chain to the top and then hurling downward at a much greater speed. Except that in this instance, the boat reached the top or the crest of the wave and would then very often belly flop down on the backside of the wave. Unfortunately, this type of occurrence dramatically increases the potential for structural damage.

The boat was thirty-eight feet in length, which gave me my only means of actually judging the size of the waves. The waves on average were in excess of forty feet—some even larger. Again, crawling up the front side was slow, and now each time we began to climb, I prayed, "Oh, God, help us; oh Lord, protect us; heavenly father, forgive me for my sins and trespasses." I virtually maintained this prayer for as long as the seas continued, which was probably five or six hours. I did not attempt to make ship log entries in these huge seas and probably wouldn't have been able to, anyway.

I harnessed myself in the cockpit, and I said a prayer during each wave. Being harnessed to the cockpit would prevent me from being thrown overboard. Sarah was lying on her back in the cockpit, just in front of the helm and me. When one of us was not steering, the other was on there, back in the cockpit well. The best part of being in the cockpit well was that you were wedged in between both sides of the walls, which kept you secure.

All of what I have described was very bad, but the worst was this: because the seas were confused, on occasion it would be necessary to change course a bit to avoid a rogue wave, if I could see one coming. Because of the darkness—there was no moon and no stars—the only light came from my running lights. Running lights really are meant to allow the boat to be visible to other boats, not to light an area in front of the boat. Beyond the bow or any part of the boat—anything beyond about ten feet or so—was total blackness for three hundred and sixty degrees.

I had just come down off the crest of another huge wave. Suddenly, I felt the rudder start to vibrate, something like the way a car feels at about forty or fifty miles per hour, when the wheels are out of balance and the car shakes. I finally realized that the boat had been struck by a rogue wave. The boat then, hurled broadside down the wall of the wave, which was very distressing, to say the least. The vibration came from the resistance of the rudder, which was perpendicular to the wall of water. I concluded this within seconds, which seemed more like minutes.

After I realized what had happened, I found myself in the trough of the wave, at the very bottom. At this point, I could look up and see the two huge walls of water that I sat between, each about thirty-five to forty feet high. I said, "Oh God in heaven, God of the universe, God of all that is, I beseech thee, oh heavenly father, to help us. Oh Lord, please hear my plea." Until this day, I do not know how we managed to extricate ourselves. I pushed the throttle all the way forward at full power, attempting to plow through the trough of these two huge walls of water. I can only say that it must have been divine intervention that saved us from being buried under those two enormous waves.

Chapter 6

Spiritual Events and Reality

How many concrete, provable, documented spiritual events would there ever be? Are the spiritual experiences that people have had mostly if not all subjective? Those people are the ones who had the experiences. Did they truly have those experiences, or were the events hallucinations? The experiences certainly seemed real to the individuals, but were they?

Most of the time, we certainly know the difference between dreams and reality. Do we then know the difference between spiritual events, hallucinations, and reality; in the same way we know the difference between dreams and reality? Is a vision or a spiritual event that one might see a part of physical reality? Also, would the beholder be the only one who was able to view the event? Would the event even occur if an individual were not alone? Conceivably, we all probably have the ability to experience events of a spiritual nature, but I believe that nearly all of the time, the events occur when we are alone. Most of the time, they occur when an individual is in a deeper spiritual place in his or her life, with the mind open enough to have the ability to have such an experience.

Is what we see real, or perhaps part of another dimension? Is our awareness of supernatural events part of our reality, or a different-dimensional reality? Can others see what we experience, even if they are not at a similar place of consciousness? I believe, based upon a certain set of circumstances of individuals, that it is possible, but not likely.

In order to have light enter a dark room, one must raise the shades or open the curtains. Light is there, and it exists outside the room, but is blocked by the drawn shades or curtains. To experience spiritual growth, depth, and a degree of awareness, people must open their minds and hearts to the possibility of just about anything occurring.

Anything is possible. The realm of imagination is the realm of possibility. Put the ego aside; the egoist mind is the doubtful mind. If we think of all that is—the planet, the universe, the integrated complexities of man and existence—then anything is possible. Doubt is a negative force that inhibits one's ability to function at a high potential of productivity or awareness. Doubt is detrimental to us and the archenemy in achieving success. It can affect other emotions and can discourage and inhibit achievement. We must learn to control and minimize doubt. Positive thought, trust in God, trust in oneself, and hard work will ultimately perpetuate our aspirations. As Jesus said, "What we think, so shall it be." There is more truth to this statement than we can ever imagine.

Based on the law of attraction, we actually have the ability to manifest that which we desire and to reject that which we do not desire. "What we think, so shall it be." For things we might desire in our lives, it is the repetition of the thoughts about what we wish to occur that shall bring those desires to fruition. (Please refer to chapter 3 on meditation and the law of attraction.) Law of attraction is the means of manifesting what we desire in our lives through the repetition of the thought, as though our desire already existed in our life.

I had an interesting experience during the winter of 2003 when I was staying at my daughter's home until my new residence was available. Her place was a two-story home, and I stayed for a week or two in a bedroom on the first floor. One night while lying in bed, I began to smell the most overwhelming fragrance of flowers—lilacs, I believe. It was January in the Midwest, so I knew the smell did not come from outside and there were no live flowers in my room or in the house. However, I did know that this experience could signify an angelic presence, and I knew of no other explanation. Two or three nights passed, and it happened again. Then it happened a third and final time.

I had experienced the same fragrance of lilacs in an apartment I had lived in about three years before staying with my daughter. I experienced the fragrance again in my current home, with my wife, Pam, who also detected the same smell of lilacs. Nothing more as far as any unusual experiences occurred other than the smell of lilacs in these particular instances.

Sometimes it is important to know that the angels are there. They may stroke us with the scent of flowers. We might be alone, and suddenly, we will smell beautiful flowers where there could not possibly be any. I suspect we know then that it is the angels reaching out to us. The mysterious scent of flowers is a frequent sign that angels give to us. The sense of smell is the sense least likely blocked by our ego as it tries to tell us that an experience is not possible. Somehow it is much more difficult to restrain or stop the sense of smell than other senses.

Angels are messengers from spirit, allowing us a greater understanding and connection to God. The word "angel" comes from the Greek *angelos,* which is the word for messenger. Angels are also part of our consciousness, representing planes beyond thought. The human mind needs to recognize form, so the light of spirit takes on the physical form of an angel to encourage direct communion with God. I somehow know now that the direct experiences with the angels precipitated in me a greater depth and connection to God as universe.

Another of the most extraordinary events I have ever had, occurred when my previous wife and I had begun seeing a marriage counselor. After our first session of the week, which we attended together, we would see the counselor separately, weekly, each of us twice a week. We had been seeing the counselor for two months or so.

On Tuesday, it was my session with the counselor. It was about ten in the morning, I believe, in February or March of 1987. When I finish with the description, you will know why this event is still so vivid in my mind.

The session began with a discussion of the kind of relationship I had been having with my wife during the past few days. About fifteen or twenty minutes into the session, I began to experience the most peculiar sensation. It was similar to the feeling we have sometimes if we stand up too quickly and the blood rushes to the head, causing a feeling of faintness. But I was sitting and not standing, and the sensation was accompanied by a tingling feeling throughout my body. The next moment, I realized that I felt like I was somewhere else, and I was out of my body.

The lightheadedness was gone and I was hovering perhaps about six or seven feet directly above myself, looking down. I could see myself sitting on the sofa but from a vantage point directly above. I could see the top of my head, shoulders, and legs. I could also see Norma, the counselor, as I looked down at her. I was part of the ceiling and the space in the room above. I could talk, and I did, and Norma said it seemed as though my voice was coming from everywhere. She knew, somehow, that something was happening even before I said anything. I mentioned to her what was occurring, and she said she could feel a different presence in the room. She also mentioned she had had a cold, but that it was now gone.

While I was in this out-of-body state, I felt exceptionally uninhibited and almost omnipotent, an ineffable feeling of total peace and being a part of space, with no physical presence and, of course, no body weight. I felt like an androgynous, intellectual or spiritual presence. This astonishing sense of freedom and ubiquitous presence, of consciousness without a body, is so overwhelmingly indescribable. I was in two places at the same time. I could still feel my physical body on the sofa but could feel nothing other than the body itself. Simultaneously, I experienced the sensation of being an intelligent, out-of-body presence or spiritual form, part of the space in the room and beyond. There are just simply no words in the English language to describe how I actually felt.

This out-of-body presence was with this sense of being present everywhere in the room and beyond. While my spiritual presence seemed to be everywhere, with no particular focal point, the point of view I had was from the ceiling above my physical body. I felt, after a few minutes, that something else should occur; I was waiting for something else to happen, but it did not. As fast as this experience came about, it was over quickly, perhaps within three or four minutes. I somehow felt that I should have learned more from the event, and I wanted to have experienced more. To this day, I still vividly recall the experience and how it has changed my life. I was so fortunate to experience a glimpse of the eternal, and this total intimacy with the divine made me feel so blessed. I now felt I had a true example from experience that God does exist and is not simply part of a belief system.

When this experience ended, I felt such overwhelming peace and had infinitely more patience within. My counselor and I starred at each other without saying a word, which seemed like several minutes. She began to shed tears, and I joined her. Again, I do not know what else to say or how to describe how I felt. I suspect, as I write these words now, that what I felt was an inimitable and uniquely heightened awareness. I felt so different with this new awareness. I felt almost as though I had been elevated to a higher plane of consciousness, and later that day, I realized that I had been. That's the only way I can describe the situation. I experienced an overwhelming general awareness, patience, understanding, and compassion and felt an extreme degree of peace about myself.

For a while, I did not seem to have normal desires for things like eating, drinking, reading, watching television, or making love. I had been smoking cigarettes before that, and I had no desire to smoke anymore. I forced myself to eat and drink, knowing I needed to do so. I had loved classical music before this change, and I loved it now even more. I seemed to be almost in a trancelike state. Perhaps the best way to describe how I felt is that I had all of my bodily functions, and my five senses were normal, but I felt so different relating to my state of mind.

I am truly not insinuating that I became any more of a person than what I had been. Probably the best way to describe how I felt and looked is that it was similar to a scene in the movie *The Ten Commandments*. Do you recall when Charlton Heston portrayed

Moses, and was leading the Hebrews out of Egypt and the clutches of the Pharaoh? He was descending the historic Mount Sinai with the two tablets of the Ten Commandments, one in each arm. Do you remember his face, his expression, and the look about him? His was the look you would imagine one might have after meeting God. That is the kind of look and the demeanor I had then. Moses in the movie, had just experienced an audience with God, and his face appeared to show this. How does one's facial expression look after being with God? This is the most descriptive way to describe my state, with no intentions of alluding to anything other than how I felt then.

This elevated state of mind lasted for some time. I was very different, and my wife and children noticed the difference. They questioned why I was acting so strangely. I was not only being fatherly to my children, who were about six and eight, but to my wife as well. I seemed to have this elder fatherly attitude toward virtually everyone I knew and met.

Although I seemed to function normally, both my own actions and everything around me seemed to move much more slowly. I seemed to talk and move at a slower pace. I had this continual, overwhelming degree of calm, patience, understanding, and compassion about me. I suspect that how I felt was due to what I had experienced during the out-of-body event. What I felt was an elevated plane or higher level of consciousness, which was very obvious. My perception of reality was different; I seemed cognizant of so much more. I experienced a general awareness that was sharper than as a razor's edge.

If we have trouble seeing, and most everything is somewhat of a blur, we put on our glasses, and then all is clear. Probably the best way to describe what had happened was that my reality, which had appeared to be clear before, was now much clearer. I suspect it was this higher level of consciousness, which enabled deeper clarity of reality. I felt a depth to things, a unique awareness of reality, possibly through having encountered a deeper dimension. The only one who knew about the experience was the marriage counselor. I somehow felt afraid, and I did not want to mention the experience to anyone else. I suspect that I thought that no one would believe me and that everyone would think I was losing touch.

The overwhelming experience of peace and calm continued to filter through my body. I owned a bakery business at this time, and I found it somewhat difficult to conduct myself in a productive, businesslike manner. I regret now that I did not permit myself to stay in this state of mind. I could not seem to function as required to remain in the kind of reality I needed. This state of mind was so pleasurable, and elating that it was difficult to return to a normal state of being. So I did everything I could possibly think of to find a way to extricate myself from this state of mind. I started smoking and listening to rock music instead of classical. I forced myself to have a drink, namely scotch. I started exercising vigorously, watching television, and deliberately being opinionated and argumentative with others. I did anything I could imagine to try to enable a return to a normal plane of existence. It's incongruous that I considered all of the previous acts I had performed to be a normal plane of existence! Yet all of those things are a reality in most of our so-called normal lives.

The return really did not seem too appealing. Gradually, I started descending and returning, and in a matter of days, I was back to what most of us call a state of normality. To this day, I regret returning; I somehow feel that there was a destiny I circumvented. "God, what have I done?" However, if it was in fact a destiny, I shall meet it once again. Meanwhile, I felt glad, but simultaneously, I felt immensely much more sad.

It's ironic that so many people live their daily lives based on all those allegedly normal acts. Now that I recognize the stark distinction between the higher level of consciousness and the so-called normal plane of existence, it is regrettable and distressing that I did return. What seemed important to me at the time was also selfish by not accepting the higher plane of existence. By returning to normality, which was, I suspect, because of my business and how my distinctively different demeanor affected it. Returning was also selfish of me in the sense that I chose to disregard this gift of the higher level of consciousness and return to a so-called normal existence.

Would it be reasonable to assume, regarding the dysfunction of the so-called normality mentioned above and other questionable situations or belief systems in society, that they exist due to distorted or unrealistic ideology some people maintain? Simply because an ideology may be true and dictates the manner in which many people function and live their lives, that does not insure its moral validity and make it the proper course to follow. Influenced by the opinions of people in society, we often find ourselves living in that society by adhering to sometimes questionable or perhaps incorrect philosophies. Do we assume that the values of the majority dictate the correct paths to follow? Mass belief in a value system does not ensure that the system is moral. Mass belief in communism, socialism, war, sterilization, the violation of a country's constitution, abortion, and violation of human rights, to name a few, are not considered moral or correct principles by many. There always seems to be this dichotomy in society between what is true and moral and what is not. Truth should be derived through investigative research in order to determine as much factual data as possible about a subject before formulating a belief.

Besides striving to have a greater awareness of truth, we should also have an awareness of the ethics and morality of the truth. Just because an event, situation, or ideology is true, that does not necessarily ensure its morality. Belief systems may obscure truth and may influence society, which in turn perpetuates mass belief. It is important to maintain an understanding and awareness of why we believe what we believe. Have our beliefs been based on parental or spiritual guidance, on initial and current personal environmental associations, on governmental doctrines, or on educational influence? How much of the aforementioned has influenced our belief system? How much have we as individuals scrutinized the actual truth and the morality of an alleged truth in relation to what we believe and how we live our lives? Ideologies and doctrines that contain truths do not necessarily insure the morality of the truth. Too often, our perceptions of a subject are influenced by society rather than by our own individual assessments. This can lead to our permitting society to claim superiority and ultimately to the obscuring of our own individual choices regarding morality.

I believe God, as universe, and we humans are all interconnected as one entity. The awareness of this fact may be more obvious to some of us than to others, due to how open people's minds are and where they are in their levels of consciousness. To gain realization of a connectedness to our source, to God, one must have an unrestrained open mind, which means a self-observed psyche, unlocked to God, to oneself, and to an expansion of traditional values. In essence, this means an augmented level of integrity incorporated into our daily lives. We must learn to listen and to recognize what our heart says to us, as subtle as the voice may be.

God as universe cannot reveal itself; it will remain a belief system for some of us, and a knowing for others. Until we are able to have self-observed minds, find quiet time, meditate, pray, or be a party to spiritual events, we will have and maintain a belief system rather than an actual knowing. Traveling beyond a belief system to a knowing will necessitate a focus on ourselves and on God as universe, as described above. I am so blessed and fortunate to know God as universe, not through belief systems but rather through personal events. My belief system has not been reinforced but has rather been replaced with an actual knowing of God as universe, through the experiences and awareness described in this book.

What we seek and what we desire *will* come to fruition, with trust in ourselves, in God, in hard work, and in our belief that it will get us there!

Section 3

Meditation

Chapter 7

Meditation Defined

What we know of the history of meditation is quite vague. Meditation is rarely taught in schools, and historical information on the practice is usually passed down orally through the generations. The word itself comes from the Latin word *meditari*, which means, "to concentrate."

Patanjali, an Indian yogi, is accepted by most as the father of meditation, contrary to the belief of those who associate Buddhism with the beginning of meditation. Zen Buddhism made its appearance in the seventh century AD. Patanjali was a physician who is said to have lived between 500 BC and 200 AD in northern India. However, it's not possible to know his exact dates. His writings, called *sutras*, give advice on how to live morally and how to use yoga daily. Almost two hundred of these sutras were collected into one of many books containing his writings, *The Yoga Sutra of Patanjali*.

The 1960s saw a rise in the acceptance of meditation worldwide, as the practice was now brought to the mass populations. Maharishi

Mahesh Yogi brought transcendental meditation to the world, likely due to his famous relationship with the Beatles.

Western traditions that have also used meditation, including Christian mystics, Theresa of Avila, a prominent Spanish mystic, Carmelite nun and Roman Catholic saint that achieved amazing insight through meditation. The Sufi Muslim sect is another example, as they enter a meditative state to contemplate Allah.

Although there are many questions as to when meditation originated, there is no question as to its benefits.

Meditation is a mental quest and inner journey to know oneself. Meditation can also enable a means by which we can evoke a state of mind that facilitates a connection to our source, our God. So meditation is both a way to access a means of bonding with the universe, one's creator, and a way to discover new characteristics of oneself. The insight gained through meditation is not instantaneous; however, the state of the individual determines the duration of time needed to begin to experience new frontiers.

So often, we in so many instances are not aware of or do not have the desire to attempt to connect to our source. And so many of us, so often, are not aware or do not have the desire to know more about ourselves. Do we have the desire? If not, will we ever attempt a connection to our source through some psychological means or an induced meditative state?

Meditation can escalate our consciousness and awareness about ourselves, can create balance in our lives, can help us develop a stronger connection to God as universe, and can perhaps help us to actually find answers that we could not have conceived in a non-meditative state. Balance through meditation creates harmony in our lives in the same way that a musical instrument sounds so much better when it is in proper tune. Meditation is a means to tune our lives and ourselves! When you are finished with your meditation, you will feel refreshed and invigorated. Meditation can also be an aid in training and a path in enlightening one's mind.

Have you ever found yourself in an almost involuntary, trancelike stare, your eyes fixed to an object? This experience could occur at work, at home, or virtually anywhere. When this state occurs, it feels more difficult to remove one's focus from the object than it would be under normal circumstances. Because we find it to be so pleasurable, relaxing, and peaceful, we do not want to stop the stare state we are in. This state of mind can possibly be construed as a kind of involuntary meditation or a semi-hypotonic state of mind. We are able to speak and carry on a conversation. We are able to remove ourselves from this state at any time, even though we are reluctant to do so. This stare state of mind is a classic indicator of how meditation may help us feel relaxed and pleasurable. Though, of course, in true meditation, one ultimately acquires a greater depth of peace, awareness, balance and understanding.

A 2007 study by the US government found that nearly twenty million people had practiced meditation within the previous twelve months. Since the 1960s, meditation has been the focus of increasing scientific research. Serious research into meditation began in the early 1930s and increased dramatically during the 1980s. Over one thousand published research studies on various methods of meditation have linked it to changes regarding blood pressure, brain activity, and other bodily functions. Meditation has been used in a significant number of clinical studies as a method of stress and pain reduction.

Secular forms of meditation were introduced in India in the 1950s, and then these forms were introduced into the United States and Europe in the 1960s as Western versions of Hindu meditative techniques. Rather than focusing on spiritual growth, secular meditation emphasizes the reduction of stress, relaxation, and self-improvement. Both spiritual and secular forms of meditation have been the subjects of scientific study.

Meditation can give you a sense of calm, peace, and balance that benefit both your emotional well being and your general health. Moreover, these benefits do not end when your meditation session ends. Meditation can help carry you more calmly through your day. When you meditate, you clear away the information surplus that builds up every day and contributes to your stress. Meditation can ultimately create more awareness and a greater insight and understanding toward others and of oneself.

Most religions include a form of meditation as part of their practice. Buddhism, Christianity, Hinduism, Islam, Judaism, and many of the New Age religions include forms of meditation, but many other religions do as well. If meditation appears in no other form, virtually all religions include it at least in the form of prayer.

The following are a few different popular types of meditation:

Guided Meditation. Sometimes called guided imagery or visualization, with this method of meditation, you form mental images of places or situations you find relaxing. Try to use as many senses as possible, such as sights, smells, and sounds. A guide or teacher may also lead you through the meditative process.

Mindfulness Meditation. This form is based on being mindful, or having an increased awareness and approval of being in the present moment. You expand your consciousness and awareness. You focus on what you experience during meditation, such as watching your breath. You can monitor your thoughts and emotions, but let them pass without opinion. Buddhist monks use this practice as a way of self-awakening.

Transcendental Meditation. You repeatedly use a mantra, such as a word, a sound, or a phrase. Eliminate all thoughts from your mind as much as possible. You focus exclusively on your mantra to achieve a state of faultless stillness. Engage in unrelenting chanting of the mantra, until a trancelike state of mind is realized. This is useful for those who are easily unfocused, as chanting a mantra will avert your mind from wandering. If you are meditating alone, you may use any word or phrase that works for you. You can repeat it either aloud or silently in your head.

Mantra Meditation. In this type of meditation, similar to Transcendental Mdeditation you speak aloud and repeat a calming word, thought or phrase to prevent distracting thoughts. It is a means to experience God by repeating the mantra. Mantra meditation is the repetition word or groups of words, which create sound sensations directly related to, and that awaken, the love of God in our hearts and minds.

Yoga. This is a physical, mental, and spiritual practice, which originated in ancient India. The purpose is the attainment of a state of perfect spiritual insight and tranquility. You perform a series of controlled breathing and postures in order to promote a more flexible body and a controlled, calm mind. It reduces stress and enables more focus on your busy day.

Walking Meditation. You can meditate while walking down the street or around the house or even while you are running. I sometimes meditate while using the treadmill, and when my mind starts to wander, I concentrate on the movement of my body and my breathing, and I observe the feeling of my moving body parts.

Meditation is a means by which we can discover a new world without an end. It is so amazing. Have you ever thought about the universe, infinity, and space, without a beginning and without an end, just as God is without a beginning and without an end?

Meditation, too, is a place without an end, an endless world of awareness, learning, and connection through ourselves to our source, God as universe.

What would writing be like without the space between the words? It would be meaningless. What would music be without the space between the notes? It would be noise.

Then we have meditation, the quiet time and space to ourselves, a time of contemplative, introspective thought. Meditation can be a quiet time for us, the space between the actions in our daily routine. It is a time during which we can gain balance, peace, calm, and insight and reduce or eliminate stress.

Meditation is a means, by which one may transcend beyond, to a better understanding of oneself and to a balance of mind, an awareness of truth, and a peace through tranquility. Tranquility gradually increases with more meditation and permeates throughout our being.

Chapter 8

Meditation Awareness and Techniques

I t is best to begin a meditation session on an empty stomach, or at least when you have not had anything to eat or drink for at least a half an hour. You begin a meditation session with your eyes closed; you may find yourself with a haphazard "monkey mind," rehashing daily events. Let them elapse, like a movie coming to its end. Then, when the movie is over, your mind is open to universal events. The more you meditate, the less time you will need for the monkey mind or for the recollection of daily events to end. Then, there is this openness for whatever might be in the cosmos.

I find that after the monkey mind, I began to see colors, primarily ultraviolet and chartreuse. The ultraviolet manifests in different intensities, and it may be by itself or may have a perimeter of two or three shades of chartreuse. Their shapes are not uniform but random— the shape that a single drop of color would take in a clear pool of water. The shape would have no symmetry—simply a random shape. It would disperse to whatever avenue was open. What I see is an intense patch of color, sometimes moving away and other times moving toward me. The sense or feeling at this time is very relaxed, but I would describe my state as being extremely peaceful with tenderness or love. I sometimes feel, during this period of color, that something else is trying to occur, but that it has not done so yet. It may perhaps be that I am just not ready for it to take place.

"When the student is ready, the teacher will appear," as the Buddhist proverb says. However, I believe that you are your own teacher, and that the self is the teacher of you. With an open, self-observed mind and a tranquil enough soul, the teacher will appear—you will appear. You will teach yourself through your own inherent, self-observed observations. You are your own guru. We all must learn how to learn, make harmonious decisions, and be motivated to change. A self-observed mind involves being aware of your own thoughts and the significance they may have for others and for you. Through meditation and deep contemplation, you can find new consciousness. You will open doors to awareness that relates to the different aspects of life such as emotions of, understanding, and compassion. Elevation of the elements of love, peace, and joy automatically enables a higher degree of consciousness than the current baseline in most individuals. Meditation will ultimately result in the manifestation of the peace, awareness, and morality that are so essential in a fulfilled existence.

I was visiting my son, Jason, in Boulder, Colorado, for about a week. Jason also practices meditation and teaches psychology at Naropa University in Boulder. It was a Sunday night, and he asked if I would be interested in attending the kirtan-chanting event with him. What an uplifting experience! **Kirtan**, one of the oldest sacred music traditions of the world, helps the mind to become quiet, peaceful, and open to experience and more insight. Kirtan practice involves chanting hymns or mantras to the accompaniment of instruments such as the harmonium, the two-headed mrdanga, the pakawaj drum, and karatal hand cymbals.

Meditation does not come easy for many people. So that is where kirtan offers another method. Without the work of mentally quieting the mind, kirtan can carry us naturally to a place of quiet, to stillness. One of the oldest sacred music traditions on the planet, the kirtan call-and-response chanting method comes to us from India. Using ancient Sanskrit mantras, the kirtan calls upon sacred energies, which produce a quiet mind, remove obstacles, and bring us to the center of our being. Check for a kirtan group in your city to complement your meditation or perhaps seek out a different type of meditation.

Another instance, which started in Boulder stemmed from a meeting with a woman named Michelle, a very well known and respected astrologer who gave me an astrological reading later that month when I was back in St. Louis. One of the most outstanding predictions she made was that in the near future, in the course of meditation, I would see a five-pointed white star. When I saw the star, I should merge with it, because I would then be merging with the galaxy.

About six or seven months after returning to St. Louis from Boulder, during a morning meditation, I saw a five-pointed white star. There it was, as clear as day. I was in a state of shock; at first, I was just so stunned that I was frozen, even in my meditative state. I had not thought about the star for months, and now there it was. I was so excited; I tried desperately to bring the star to me and then me to the star, but to no avail. It remained in sight for about a minute, and then it was gone. I suspected that I had just tried too vigorously to achieve the merge. When I see the intense ultraviolet and chartreuse colors in meditation, I attempt to merge, and I usually do.

Later, after contacting Michelle about the event, I realized that I had actually automatically merged with the star, simply by having the opportunity to observe it. Merging with the five-pointed star facilitated awareness and a heightened intimacy with the divine, according to Michelle, and I felt this to be so. Michelle stated, "This means physically, you stopped breath and you were supported by divine energy. Your ego has moved beyond time and space."

What happened makes more sense now, and it explains my realization of knowledge of subjects I have not studied, knowledge that I never learned but now know somehow, which is a good part of the reason I am writing this book. I also find that I have realized more patience, understanding, and sensitivity on a daily basis. In addition, I am so much more at peace with myself.

I have also found that I have realized more of an understanding of existentialism in previous years, through periods of intense meditation twice a day, two to four hours or more at a session when I was not working. One session I know was over six and half hours. It was difficult to move or stand afterward. Although my legs were not completely asleep, they were stiff. It took much time and stretching to regain a normal physical state after being in the half lotus position for so long.

Meditation is more effective and beneficial at sunrise and sunset when atmospheric energy is at its zenith. At these times, one has a stronger opportunity to experience greater depth and connection to the universe as God.

Currently, I now meditate twice a day for a minimum of thirty minutes per session. Some of the sessions throughout the month may be increased to much longer periods. All of the meditation sessions are followed immediately afterward by several minutes of prayer on a traditional prayer rug. My personal preference is my body prostrated; I go to my knees, with my forehead touching the carpet and my hands at the side of my head. This is an exclusive time simply to thank God for no more than God's existence and presence in and of the universe, for God's simply being. I recite, repeatedly with my forehead touching the prayer rug: *"God of heaven, God of the universe, God of all creation, and God of all that is, I thank thee, oh God, for thy being. I love thee, oh Lord."* While my head touches the carpet, many times, I feel pressure at my crown chakra, the top of my head, which usually indicates energy from the universe. Each time, I raise my torso straight up but remain on my knees for a few seconds, and then I return my forehead to the carpet. I repeat the prayer three times.

One technique I use for meditation is sitting in a half lotus position on the floor, with a firm pillow (called a *zafu*) and with my eyes closed. The half lotus position involves having my left leg crossed in front of me on the floor and my right leg crossed over the top of my left calf. If this position is too uncomfortable for you, then simply cross both legs in front of you in the way that is most comfortable. It is important to be on the floor for grounding purposes. If either of these positions is too difficult, then try sitting on a chair with both feet on the floor, touching each other.

With either position, my hands are in my lap, palms straight up, with my fingers touching and curled upward, signifying openness to God. The purpose of this position is to have all body parts touching and grounded. My back is straight and arched, relaxed but not too relaxed; I do not want to fall asleep. The position is kind of like having all circuits closed in an electrical connection to allow the current or the energy to flow. Flip the breaker or break the connection, and the current or energy stops. Having all body parts touching closes the body circuit, which enables a stronger connection to God as universe in this meditative state. Of course, keep the eyes closed to enhance the expansion of your mind, and it is most important to be certain you are relaxed and that the area is quiet, without distractions.

Meditation can be more effective at sunrise and sunset because of the earth's energy being stronger at these periods. It is not imperative to meditate at these times, but it may give greater depth to your meditative state. In addition, if you ever have an occasion to awake in the early morning, the period around 2:00 a.m. to 3:00 a.m. could be an excellent time to meditate. At this time, in North America, most people are at rest. When people are asleep, the possibility of their minds inadvertently obstructing your morning mediation is lessened. The waking energy of their processes of thinking, speaking, and taking action can lessen your ability to achieve depth in your mediation. Think of this in terms of radio or TV stations operating in the midst of a thunderstorm. The TV and radio stations, especially the AM stations, encounter much interference and static from the lighting and thunder. When we are meditating during the day, we may have interference from the energy emitted from other awakened minds. But during the wee hours of the morning, most minds are sleeping, resulting in much less interference.

At times, the sun, moon, and gravitational changes can also have an effect. Think of how the moon creates tidal changes in the ocean. The changes can be minimal or dramatic. The moon affects the tides on the planet; when the moon is new or full, it creates both higher high tides and lower low tides. In the same way, the planets, the moon, and the sun can sometimes affect our daily demeanor and our meditation.

You have heard the expression, "It's a full moon tonight, and all the loons will be out." The gravitational changes can affect people in both negative and positive ways.

In meditation, to help you relax sooner, you should take deep, long slow breaths. These are helpful, even if they are not essential.

Meditation can be quiet, or it may be performed while chanting a mantra. A mantra is a sound, syllable, word, or group of words that may generate transformation. Many of these are in the form of sacred words or texts written in Sanskrit, the oldest classic language from India.

Hinduism, like Buddhism, often uses these sacred expressions of syllables or words because they are believed to express magical or spiritual power. These mantras are usually repeated during the course of meditation. The repetition of a mantra will usually produce a trance-like state of mind and may ultimately lead an individual to a higher state of awareness.

Two of the most traditional sounds used as mantras in the course of meditation are "Ah" and "Ohm," or "Om." "Ah" is one of the most potent mantras on the planet. It is an extremely powerful sound that is principally useful for generating compassion as a means for helping to enable the transformation of consciousness on the planet. The "Ah" sound is representative of the sound of the heart chakra, and it is the ambassador of love and compassion. Most spiritual teachers feel that the activation of the heart chakra aids in initializing higher levels of consciousness. Nearly all believe that the energy of the heart and the emitting of love is the principal and fundamental energy of the universe.

Begin at sunrise or early in the morning by taking four or five long, slow, deep breaths. After these initial deep breaths, continue with further slow deep breaths by inhaling as much air into your lungs as possible through your nose. When you have reached full capacity, exhale through your mouth while saying the mantra "Ah."

"Ahhhhhhhhhhhhhhhhhhhhhhhh." Say the protracted, resonating sound throughout, from the beginning of each exhale to the very end. Say this sound aloud at a normal or slightly above normal volume. If the meditation session lasts for, say, twenty-five minutes, gradually start lowering the volume as the allotted time begins to expire. By the time you near the end of the session, the volume should be almost at a whisper, and finally lowered to a whisper. For the last couple of minutes of the session, the sound of the exhale should be just the sound of your breath. Permit your mind to be open to anything, and do not attempt to stop any thoughts that may be unwanted. Let all that you feel in the meditation occur. If you experience an unwanted thought, observe it, and then let it go.

"Ah" is also a means of manifesting all that you may desire in your life. It reverberates with what you want in the experience. Using this mantra is an ancient method of meditation for creating and manifesting our desires into our lives. It is essential that we maintain a focus on our desires and avoid external thoughts that might contaminate and inhibit the actual focus of the intended experience. All that we desire exists already, and this form of meditation can enable us to facilitate a shift, so that which we desire can be brought to fruition.

When one has the will to capture a glimpse of the eternal, the intrepid desire to do so, and an insatiable wish for achievement, then he or she may continue the pursuit. With lack of doubt, as in the technique of the power of attraction, in the forthcoming description, it is to achieve our desires through focused meditation. The attraction of what we desire in our life is accomplished through manifesting in the course of meditation without doubt. This is achieved through the repetition of thinking our desire is already in our life which ultimately brings it to fruition. If you can have an absolute knowing without any doubt, all that you desire shall come to pass. I believe doubt is the archenemy of the purity of thought, and it inhibits the essence of all that is.

That which one desires in their life will come to fruition without doubt. It is that simple, but such simplicity is not always easily achieved. If we could only have a greater degree of positive thinking, we would lead much more optimistic and constructive lives. It is paramount that we develop positive attitudes, coupled with faith, hope, and trust in God, and apply these to situations we wish to transform. However, our fear of failure or loss can inhibit our success for change.

For manifesting that which you desire in your life, recite the protracted "Ah" mantra with deep breaths as described earlier, for at least twenty-five minutes per day for thirty days. Inhale slowly through your nose as much air as your lungs can hold, and then exhale slowly through your mouth, expelling as much air as possible until there is virtually no air left in your lungs. Repeat this practice for a minimum of twenty-five minutes for each session. In the course of the meditative state, you should actually visualize that what you are attempting to manifest already exists. It is already in your life; it is already happening. For example, I might want the general manager or presidents position in my company, or I want my sister or brother to find the kind of position they desire for their success. I want to find romantic love in my life or I want to rid myself of this dreaded disease.

In the course of the meditation, to manifest in your life that which you desire, visualize that you have actually received the promotion, that your sibling has obtained the position, you have found the romantic love of your life, or that you are now free of the medical issue. Visualize how the process of the promotion would transpire. Perhaps your boss calls you into his office and begins congratulating you; you have received the new position. He may show you your new office or tell you how pleased the company has been with your work. You meet your secretary; perhaps you have never had a secretary. He now hands you a written job description and leaves it for you to review. He says to call him with any questions. The first call you make is to your wife, husband, or friend. You are actually imagining that which you desire already exists, and you construct your own idea of how the promotion is to be manifested. Use such visualizations for your own desires as you meditate.

Repeating the process, you may even enhance the visualization, giving more detail each time; continue this technique for the duration of the session. Again, it is extremely important, when using this process for manifesting, to avoid permitting any other thoughts to appear that could contaminate your specific thought process, which is the opposite of what I mentioned earlier. Unwanted thoughts interfere with your focus on the desire that you wish to manifest. Avoid contaminated thoughts resulting from outside noise and thoughts that may enter your mind that are not related to your focus and that might interfere with your manifesting meditation. When outside thoughts do occur, release them as soon as possible to avoid contaminating your manifesting process. In addition, it is best not to discuss manifesting your desire with anyone in order to circumvent any negative opinion that could obscure or influence you, perhaps create doubt, hinder your focus, and negate your goal. Use this same technique for manifesting your sibling's success, finding romantic love, or eliminating a medical issue. If you do have any medical problems, your physician should be aware of this process prior to implementation.

In the evening, at sundown, or before bed, meditate with your eyes closed, using the mantra "Ohm." For a minimum of twenty-five minutes a day, meditate while using the same breathing techniques mentioned earlier. Now the focus is on thanking God for all you have in your life. Thank God for your health, your body, and even for your healthy organs. In addition, give thanks for the health of your family, for all your material things, and so on. Be thankful for whatever is good in your life. This entire session should be focused simply on thanking God for all you possess, even some of the bad things, which always have some good in them or can eventually become good. You can always find some good in negative circumstances.

The "Ohm" is treated in the same way as "Ah." Take a deep inhale through your nose, and with the beginning of the exhale, say, *"Ohmmmmmmmmmmmmm."* Gradually let your lips begin to touch as the "m" is said. Your lips should vibrate slightly. Again, reduce the volume gradually through the meditation until you are whispering near the end, and finally just the sound of your breath.

After the meditation is complete, but before conclusion of the session, I personally perform one final act. I visualize that I am holding the planet earth between my hands, perhaps in an area the size of a basketball. I focus on the planet and imagine it rotating, and I attempt to transfer loving energy from my heart for about thirty seconds or so in the hope that it reaches all humanity.

One of the most extraordinary meditation experiences that occurred in my life was in the mid-1990s. It was during my evening meditation, close to sundown, and I think I had been meditating for about an hour. I felt a sense of peace gradually increasing, accompanied by the most unusual kind of warmth—affection, love, tenderness, kindness, joy, and compassion, which all seemed to be rolled into one collective emotion. The closest I can come to describing the event, though this is still inadequate, is that it was the most overwhelming, awe-inspiring, vast, breathtaking, ineffable feeling. The description is simply beyond words. As the combined emotions increased, tears begin to roll down my cheeks, eventually drenching me. These tears represented perhaps the pinnacle of love, peace, and joy I was experiencing. The feelings continued to develop to an unbelievable magnitude. The entire occurrence probably lasted from two to four minutes, but truly, I cannot be certain; it could have been shorter or much longer.

Probably the most accurate way to describe the event is to say that as I write this sentence, I have goose bumps and feel a subtle vibration, and that I believe that I actually made conscious contact with God. All of these exquisite emotions at such a high level, interwoven in this superb collective bond! How awe-inspiring and incredible could any one experience ever be! I felt so blessed!

As the conscious contact began to diminish, I continued to feel the peace, but not nearly as powerfully. I felt extremely weak, as though I were drugged. I suspect that this was part of the overwhelming effect of the event. Gradually, my strength began to return, and then I attempted to digest all that had occurred. I did not know where to begin. I was in a state of awe. I had not tried in the least to make this contact; the thought had never occurred to me. It just spontaneously occurred during my normal sundown meditation. I could then deduce that this happening was further evidence that would only support the belief that awareness is not attained but rather is realized unexpectedly.

I believe that the escalation of awareness and of self-improvement through meditation is possible and achievable, but not necessarily always to the extent that I just described. However, depending upon the individual and time period, it certainly is possible. Increased awareness can eventually lead to stronger insight, balance, understanding, and peace in one's life, regardless of one's business and or lifestyle. This will facilitate a happiness and peace never before realized.

Recognition of a need for improvement in awareness, insight, balance, or understanding is critical. Once you recognize the need for improvement, then, with the proper focus through meditation, introspective thought, and dedication, you will ultimately raise your awareness, insight, and balance to higher and sustainable levels. It is important to understand that it may be difficult for some individuals to recognize that improvement is necessary. People so often do not comprehend or identify the need for improvement. Recognition of the fact that we may have issues can be difficult for some people to grasp.

Historically, our beliefs are such that we do not want to believe that we may have been incorrect about some issue or emotion. We don't want to believe that we perhaps mislead others or ourselves for so many years. The ego often deludes and obscures our judgment, preventing the proper identification of any issues we may need to deal with. The ego may simply imply that we don't necessarily need improvement or change.

When a need to improve is recognized, in a quiet place, through meditation or introspective thought, it is crucial for us to search beyond our egoist minds and to determine our *true character*. Focusing intensely and posing questions to and about ourselves can enable the truth to finally surface.

It may be necessary to focus on and penetrate on perhaps *concealed inhibitions* we may maintain, to become aware of what is needed for change. We should strive to have *open minds*, uncontaminated with egoist interference. This goal is perhaps more easily described than accomplished. But with the proper focus and determination, and with the realization that this process is going to be beneficial and successful, we can bring to the surface the negative, deep-seated egoist disillusionments. We must be prepared to recognize and accept *truths* that may be uncomfortable. Nevertheless, with the recognition and acceptance of the outcome from the above, we will ultimately facilitate truth and a freedom of the self, never before realized.

If you find this too difficult a process to obtain your goal, then perhaps therapy would help bring to the surface that which you desire to know. (Please refer to the meditation summary in this section to assist in this process.)

Meditation can correlate to dreams in the sense that what we experience in the meditative state may not be immediately remembered after the session. During either meditation or dreams, we may sometimes want to recall what occurred, but for whatever reason, we cannot retain the information; it seems to slip away from memory. However, with meditation, unlike with dreams, if God as universe considers it necessary, we will either retain or eventually recall essential thoughts from the meditation. The final realization of the deep-seated issues or inhibitions can be realized through several means, one being meditation.

Summary of Meditation

1) *Meditation can give you a sense of calm, peace, and balance that benefits both your emotional well-being and your general health.*

2) *Meditation can ultimately create more awareness, greater insight, and an understanding toward others and oneself when not in a meditative state.*

3) *Meditation is a means by which we can discover a new world without an end.*

4) *Meditation is more effective and beneficial at sunrise and sunset, when atmospheric energy is at its zenith.*

5) *It is best to begin a meditation session on an empty stomach, or at least when you have not had anything to eat or drink for at least a half an hour.*

6) *Begin a meditation session with your eyes closed; you may experience "monkey mind" and haphazardly rehash daily events until your mind is clear.*

7) *Start on the floor with a firm pillow for the mediation. Cross your legs in front of you in a half lotus, or find your own comfortable position. It is important to be on the floor for grounding purposes. If any of these positions is too difficult, then try sitting on a chair, with both feet on the ground and hands together, and palms turned upward.*

8) *It is most important to be certain you are relaxed and that the area you use is quiet and without distractions.*

9)   In meditation, to help relax you sooner, take deep, long breaths in the beginning or throughout the meditation session. These are helpful but not essential. Meditation can be quiet, or you may chant a mantra, such as "Ah" or "Ohm."

10) Meditation will ultimately manifest a peace, awareness, and balance that are essential in a fulfilled existence.

Chapter 9

Enlightenment

W hy do we believe that we understand good and evil, love and hate? The connotation and dualities of these states are emotions that can transcend to action. The emotions or thoughts must exist in order to enable the action. However, they both carry positive and negative consequences. It is obvious that good and love are positive and that bad and hate are negative. But why are they considered extremes, and why do they maintain duality?

The challenge to understanding non-duality may be that which exists beyond words, when one phrase or a word is named, paradoxically, a duality is created. For example, a declaration that all things are beautiful creates a division between "beautiful" and "not beautiful." So it is hardly a shock that non-duality is misconstrued.

Evil or hate are necessary in order to appreciate goodness. If everything on the planet was good, we would not be able to appreciate goodness. There would be no comparison and no means to appreciate without the ability to distinguish. Love and hate have the same distinguishable difference in order to appreciate the positive. To love an item we must be able to appreciate love and to distinguish, without hate the opposite we could not. Yes, no, long, short, left, right, up, down, and so on—all are examples of this principle. Light is not independent of dark; nor is long independent of short. Light is part of dark on the scale of the light spectrum. Long is a part of short on the scale of measurement. The ego creates the duality of light and dark, and long and short, as opposed to light and not light or long and not long, yes and not yes (rather than yes and no). There are no opposites in the true reality; there are only relationships. However, a positive cannot exist without the negative in our dualistic daily reality, which is our reality, as we know it.

Much of our appreciation of life is due to conflicting factors in our own realities. I say that we own our own realities. One's reality is one's perception of life, how that person perceives that which is in his or her daily existence. Duality is part of our consciousness due to ego. Our egos create our perceptions of our daily realities. A Buddhist perception is that there are five collectives: consciousness, feeling, form, thought, and choice. These five collectives, when united, give an illusion of a "self"— an illusion of duality. So with consciousness and non-consciousness, feeling and non-feeling, and so on, duality is created.

Do words create duality? Or does whatever creates the words create the duality? It is very creative but with apprehension for one to be motivated toward the development of awareness of a non-dual reality, and recognizing the I of the self, being without duality. The I is independent of duality, and the self is duality. The ego creates opposites. Opposites create duality. Therefore, the ego creates duality.

Jesus taught our born bodily recognition as being soul, not just in the sense of being immortal, but also in the eternal sense, therefore in truth, now and forever in the intimacy of communion with God, in spirit, and in the radiance of being. One of the teachings of Jesus is paraphrased as follows: "Don't you know that you are God; God is spirit. The spirit gave birth to humanity. That which is born of the spirit is the Spirit."

In a normal, so-called reality, duality exists. We are conditioned to duality, or to opposites, in the realm of what we know and perceive. Because of ego, in order for the mind to comprehend, we must distinguish between entities through duality.

Higher levels of consciousness, that is, enlightened or near-enlightened states of mind, can perpetuate a non-dual state of reality, at which point the individual has transcended to an absolute "I" of the self. There are no polarities, no opposites, no right or wrong, up or down, black or white, good or evil, and so on. A non-dual state of mind perceives no positionalities, (dictates of the ego) but just simply that which is. Different shades of white, rather than black or white. Degrees of right instead of right and wrong, we would have right and not right, height, length, opposed to up or down, we would have up and not up. Degrees of good as a replacement of good and evil, good or not good, yes or not yes opposed to yes and no. Rather than being the opposite of another, each item would have its own measurement in a non-dual state of mind and would have its own totality, as opposed to having polarity. Light was given its polarity or duality when, instead of light and not-light, the word "dark" denoted the distinguishable difference, subsequently polarity or duality.

Children are void of ego boundaries and subsequently do not encompass any duality. They only know and live in the moment. They actually experience the true reality by being one with the universe, but because of their inability to communicate, they are dependent on their parents and are unable to express this true reality. As they grow older, they begin to develop ego due to relationships with parents, family, and friends and through environmental influences.

At a higher level of consciousness (enlightened state of mind), we would have the ability to experience the world without ego. One would embrace the ultimate form of awareness, though he or she would remain significantly subordinate to avatars or superior beings like Jesus, the Buddha, Muhammad, and Krishna. This level of awareness may be realized but not attained, but through long, intense, dedicated periods of meditation, or possible spiritual events that would enhance and enable this higher state of mind. A significant reduction, if not almost a total elimination of ego, coupled with a supreme open-mindedness to God as universe, would be essential to uphold for an unknown period, in isolation. For one to acquire this higher plane or level of consciousness as described would require a retreat, and a reclusive or monastic lifestyle. This lifestyle would be critical for the near, if not total solitude that would be essential to facilitate the higher state of being. Everything would need to be removed—no cars, fax machines, computers, radio, e-mail, cell phones, television, or romance. The total solitude would be necessary, and the atmosphere would need to be void of outside distractions in order to prevent one's pure thought process from being contaminated by the actions or materialism of society.

The duration of time required would depend on the individual, on his or her degree of intense concentration, and on the person's ability to focus for an undetermined period of predominately uncontaminated contemplative thought throughout the monastic lifestyle.

Once the level of higher consciousness is realized, it may not be easy for the individual to return to a normal lifestyle because of the euphoric exhilaration he or she now experiences and the lack of the desire to return. You would feel an ineffable sense of ecstasy, a connection of being at one with God as universe. This elevated plane of existence would make it extremely difficult to return to the so-called everyday life. In this elevated state of mind, you would acquire a certain increase in levels of consciousness but would also accumulate new abilities. These would include a significantly enhanced ability to understand, a sensitivity to all that is, elevated wisdom, infinite patience, and the ability to heal.

In an attempt to return to normal living in the sense of maintaining a typical existence with friends, relatives, and others, one would need to consider the following. A person may function at a certain level in society, provided that he or she feels a strong enough desire and necessity to return; perhaps one could function at the level of a sage. This realized state of mind is virtually an absolute knowing of all that is; a purity of thought uninhibited by ego, doubt, or duality. It is the capacity to experience almost ultimate compassion, sensitivity, awareness, and a true understanding of the essence of life. It is the core or the fundamental nature of all that is—a vortex, if you will, of almost pure, uncontaminated understanding and awareness. It is the purity of essence and the essence of purity.

I have not experienced this state of mind, but the words of the description feel natural, proper, correct, and true. I can only think that the process I describe above I had to realize in the course of one of my meditative states. The process remained subconscious until it surfaced while I wrote the description of an enlightened state of mind. I just somehow had an absolute knowing, as the words flowed through my mind onto the paper, that this was a true process of at least one path to Enlightenment.

Why Do Bad Things Happen to Good People and Children?

Chapter 10

Perception and Duality

The title of this section is a question that has been asked and will be asked until such time as there is definitive proof of an answer, if there ever is. We humans generally need evidence and confirmation of something before we are able to believe. Some so-called bad or evil things can be merely our perception of those things, a perception not necessarily shared by everyone. What one person may perceive as bad, you or I may not, and vice versa. So why do bad things happen to good people? Are we even supposed to know? We may wonder, at times, why God as universe permits things such as sickness or the loss of life to occur.

Perception certainly influences our beliefs about a subject. Some people consider the ideology of Karl Marx to be good, and some believe it to be bad. Karl Marx (1818–1883) is best known as a revolutionary political writer whose works served as the basis of many communist regimes in the twentieth century. Our perception determines how we interpret, and our perceptions at times inadvertently may be combined with our desires to obscure factual data. Because an ideology is true, that does not necessarily mean we can conclude and accept its morality as a whole. Therefore, in this example, the challenge is not about the truth, but about our interpretation of the morality of the truth of Marxism. The same holds true for any occasion where we need to look at the truth of a subject versus its morality.

Have you ever heard people say, "If the world were only a different place?" A perfect world would be the existence of a world without violence, hatred, and without other negatives to deal with. How would we perceive a utopian planet? It is, in all practicality, idealistic or unrealistic.

Emotions play a key role in how we distinguish and address situations in life. If there were no evil on the planet, then there would be no test and no tribulation in our lives. If we did not have the bitter, we could not appreciate the sweet. Could people appreciate good if bad never happened to them? Would we even be able to differentiate the one without the other? If all that exists on the planet is good and pure, without any bad or evil, could life be appreciated as it is now? Would we have the same perception and outlook about life?

Suppose there was no bad or evil on the planet, and we were always happy, loving, kind, compassionate, and all the other positive attributes that give us pleasure and peace. Are we even able to comprehend these positive attributes without bad or evil, their opposites? If you have never experienced a situation, it may be difficult to form an opinion about a particular circumstance. However, even though we may never have experienced certain situations we could imagine what they would be like—driving at high speed, sailing, fighting, taking a twelve-hour plane ride, bungee jumping, hunting, shooting a gun, parachuting, and so on.

Nevertheless, can you imagine how the world would be without bad or evil existing? Everything, that exists on the planet simply being good, pure, and pleasurable, without the existence of any negativity. If all that existed on the planet were good without any evil, with no negative acts ever occurring, how would we perceive life? There would be no wars, no military, no crime, no police, no lawyers, no disputes, no courts, no fires, no firefighters, no paramedics, no emergencies, no disease, no doctors, no health organizations, no insurance companies, no charities, no entity needed to counteract evil, no negativity, and no help agencies. Society would have a fundamentally and radically different structure; a world without any emotions, it would perpetuate a totally and extraordinarily different perception of life. We would have lost our individuality without the existence of emotions, in a society without bad or evil, which are the common denominators for virtually all-negative emotions without their opposites. The nonexistence of negativity would also mean the nonexistence of love, peace, and joy, without their comparisons to distinguish differences. Emotions would be virtually non-existent without their opposites. Members of the human race would likely function in virtually an identical manner. All people, in effect, would be the same in demeanor and attitude. Any emotion remaining would be infinitesimal and unnoticeable and would achieve little difference in people's performance—hence, no individuality.

It is extremely difficult, if not impossible, to imagine the world described earlier without the polarities. To attempt to imagine this state is likely futile; the mind cannot comprehend what it is not conditioned to realize, know, and accept. We are so accustomed to polarity and to opposites that enable us to differentiate and, subsequently, to appreciate.

Without bad or evil, would we have a need for hope, faith, trust, and prayer? They would be unnecessary and likely undesirable, if they even existed. Would our desires even be the same? If there were no sickness, how long would life be? Would we even grow old? Could we even die? How large would the world population be? Could we ever feel joy without sorrow, or pleasure without knowing pain and suffering? Would we be able to appreciate goodness without being able to compare it to its opposite? I think not. Good, bad and evil would not have the same definition they have now and likely would not exist.

"Good" as an emotion, and even as a word, would likely not even survive. Goodness would not give us the joy that we experience without our knowing bad. We could not appreciate and know good as an emotion without bad being available as an opposite. Good would not have the same significance or definition. Would not the meaning of good without evil be much more dispassionate, less gratifying? Would the planet, without bad or evil, only having goodness present, perpetuate a situation devoid of almost any emotions we currently have? Would the absence of evil change our emotions? Would "good" simply be ordinary life, without comparisons or opposites? Good would not have the same description or label it currently does. How would we describe feeling good or being in a good mood or being a good person without evil or bad as a comparison? I suspect good may simply be called "life," or "being," or another depiction of existence.

Would the lack of good necessitate a new and different interpretation of life and meaning? Would we need a replacement of the word "good" to denote a different way to appreciate life? Or would the lack of the word "good" or the state of mind we know as good perpetuate a void in which we had no appreciation of life? With no bad or evil, we could not hate. How would a scenario with no hatred, no bad, and no evil affect us? Without emotions, would we even have any physical sensations left? If we did have physical sensations, would what we experience in the sensation characterize anything anymore, or would there even be sensations? Would the lack of evil and bad be utterly inconceivable?

If we had any emotions left, would they even be the same? I think they would be dramatically different. Could we even feel and know joy anymore, without sorrow as a distinguishable comparison? Could we feel and know peace without disagreement or war, or pleasure without pain? Virtually no emotion would have the same significance—and would emotions even exist? If emotions in a very different world we know were nonexistent or limited, what could we experience? For example, if I would say the phrase "I am so happy today" in a society without polarities or opposites, I could not really feel happy because I could not feel sad. We need to know sad in order to know and be happy. Would the lack of emotions not change our perception of life and existence? Does the scenario generated above suggest that we need emotions or opposites like good and bad, or joy and sorrow, in order to understand, recognize value and appreciation, and distinction in life? I feel this may be the reason the world is what it is. It is my belief that one reason we have discord, disease, and death is to appreciate life.

There are people who choose to be good because of their belief that they will receive a reward for being good, either from others or from God. This type of goodness obviously does not have the same significance as the type demonstrated by those who choose good simply because they have the desire to do so without expectations. What moral beliefs do we possess, and how do they relate to our perception of life?

Those people who are philanthropic with the expectation of some type of reward for their gift do not understand the meaning of giving and understanding.

Why do bad things happen to good people? Is there such a thing as justice on the planet? I quit smoking twelve years ago. Why do I have COPD? Is it God's fault? Or is it instead because I smoked for thirty-five years? I cannot blame God because I chose to smoke cigarettes. God is not responsible for my disease; I am. Someone who drinks alcohol excessively may have cirrhosis of the liver. It is not God's fault. If someone has clogged arteries from too much fat and lack of exercise, is it God's fault? I do not think so. If someone is extremely overweight, resulting in a heart condition, that is not God's fault. If someone who loves sweets has diabetes, is it God's fault? A person who drives an unsafe car and has an accident because the brakes were bad—is it God's fault? What about the intoxicated driver crossing the double yellow line and causing a head-on collision—God's fault? What about the innocent victims who paid a price—perhaps with their lives—because of a drunk driver? Can we blame God? Should God stop every driver who is intoxicated from crossing the double yellow line? Why should God stop at just drunk drivers? Why not also simply have God stop a driver who loses control, helping him or her to avoid another car? What about other types of accidents? Perhaps God should stop them all. How about medication that was prescribed for us that had certain side effects, which may have caused an even more serious problem? The reasons mentioned earlier could be some reasons why bad things happen to good people, sometimes because of our own neglect of ourselves, or sometimes due to simply being in the wrong place at a given time, which may not be any fault of our own. Perhaps we contracted a disease that as far as we know is no fault of our own.

Is there a specific reason for any negative occurrences? Let's do a bit more investigation!

Let's consider the innocent people that perish in earthquakes, hurricanes, and other natural disasters, like the tsunami of December 26, 2004, in Thailand that killed over 230,000 people. The epicenter was off the west coast of Sumatra, Indonesia. I would suspect that the majority of the victims had done nothing to deserve this fate. Could the only explanation be that this is God's method of a cleansing of the planet? It is difficult to accept this disaster or any disaster, regardless of this reason or any other. We know people died because of the tsunami, which was caused by an earthquake, which was caused by the movement of the tectonic plates below the earth's surface. But what caused the movement of the tectonic plates? Was the cause of the movement nature—perhaps the cause was previous underground nuclear testing—or did the event spontaneously occur for no specific reason? Should there be a cause for everything that occurs? Or in this instance, was God responsible for this horrific event for some purpose—or for no purpose whatsoever? Was God responsible for the Holocaust that killed six million Jews? Or was it in fact the responsibility of the governments of the world to stop Hitler from marching across Europe in his murderous rampage? I could, of course, go on and on with other examples. It seems as though we can either find a reason or justify a negative action or events through assumption for virtually anything that occurs, if we desire and strive to do so— with perhaps one exception.

Chapter 11

Is Destiny Why Bad Things Happen?

*W*hy *do bad things happen to children?* Let's examine some possible reasons other than what was mentioned earlier. We can find a justification for virtually anything bad that occurs on the planet, with at least one exception. Can we justify and explain pediatric oncology wards? These innocent and, in many instances, helpless children have done nothing to deserve this fate. Are stricken children too good for this world? Is that why God takes them away from us? Why would a benevolent God permit a child to suffer? Do children suffer in order for science to find a means to stop the suffering of others? If there is such a thing as justice, I certainly do not think it is directed to these kids.

Why do bad things happen to children? Perhaps we just do not understand God as universe. Each human has choice, and much of one's choice may determine one's destiny. Does the way we act and conduct ourselves precipitate our fate and that of others dear to us?

113

Is there a penance we pay for our actions, or are bad things that happen strictly random?

What about young children, perhaps less than five years old? Is it their fate to succumb to a dreaded disease, which is certainly not a fate the children deserve. What could they have done at this early age to deserve this destiny if there is such a thing called justice? Is it a karmic fate resulting from a negative previous lifetime? Even if it is, children are not aware and are not able to realize that this may be a chastisement stemming from a previous life. Or are they? At a very young age, could they actually be aware of experiencing justified punishment? They cannot recollect a previous life, even if they did have one. Therefore, is this fate indiscriminate, due simply to random selection?

Is it perhaps a punishment for parent's current or past life that his or her child is now plagued with this fate? Did parents do something in their lives that perpetuated this negative scenario for their child? Is this a reprisal on the parents for an act they committed against another person? Are the parents aware of any sins that could justify their child's suffering? Why do these dreadful events happen to parents and children who do not appear to deserve punishment? Is there something called justice? Or are all occurrences simply random courses of events? Is there a grand design to all that is and all that occurs in the universe?

On the other hand, the disease the child has may result from negative energy created by a vibration in the child's household during the embryonic trimesters. Before birth, if negative energy and despair is displayed in the home, through verbal or physical abuse by the parents, this energy can be carried or transferred to the embryo; hence the possible contribution to the child's physical disease. A mother or father smoking, drinking alcohol, or taking drugs before childbirth is also usually detrimental to the health of the embryo.

Children at a young age, usually between infancy and three years old are being in the moment, and open to the universe because of their stark alertness to reality. They are not conscious of yesterday or tomorrow, only of the present moment. This enables a distinct and elevated clarity of reality, without ego, however with awareness of positive and negative energy, but without the ability to distinguish, understand, or speak. A child can experience moods and distinct frames of mind with an accelerated intuitive awareness, yet without the ability to communicate or discern. This is similar to the feeling we adults sometimes have when we are aware of something not feeling correct, yet do not know what it is or why. Adults' reality by comparison is rather obscure because of ego and duality without near the clarity of infants and children. We may have a feeling about something, either positive or negative, with no particular cause except our intuition or sense about it.

This is the kind of sense or feeling I am referring to with children's elevated clarity. In a negative situation, children have awareness or a sense of something not feeling correct, but rather feeling not only wrong but also very negative. So I believe that negative emotions displayed by parents can and do affect the embryo, in the same way very young children from infancy and older, can be affected emotionally and physically by dysfunctional acts in households because of their keen awareness.

Is there a lesson the parents should learn? If so, what would the lesson be? They would certainly suffer from the fact that their child has a disease and faces possible loss of life. Was this a price for the parents to pay, for whatever reason, whether or not they are aware of it? On the other hand, did they do absolutely nothing to justify paying this kind of price? Would either instance justify the sickness or the loss of a child?

Why do bad things happen to good people and children? Are we even supposed to know why? We know what could possibly cause bad things to happen to good people, as indicated in some of the examples mentioned earlier. Just because we, as observers, are not aware of a so-called bad act does not mean it has not occurred. However, this still leaves the question about what kind of action constitutes a bad act that would justify the retribution inflicted on a child. If a bad act in fact perpetuates reprisals, is the suffering random and spontaneous, or does it stem from one of the sources described earlier?

Should a good and just God as universe only help children with cancer who are two to four years old, or should help be extended to children from five to fifteen years old? When should God draw the line for children not getting cancer? Should God help one-year-olds to twenty-year-olds? Should God stop cancer in those of all ages? Should God even stop at cancer? What about multiple sclerosis? At what ages should God cure or stop the contracting of this disease, or of any disease or sickness, for that matter? If a disease is caused by genetics, should God intervene and abolish all the negative genes?

Why do bad things happen to children? Is it because the child's ultimate destiny is not part of the grand design of things? Perhaps his or her simple existence was a contribution to the family through the love and joy that existed while the child was here. Alternatively, does disease strike children and adults for not necessarily any reason or fault of their own, but strictly as random events? I know you do not want to hear that "the Lord works in mysterious ways." Nothing can replace a life that has been lost, and no one can know the degree of sorrow and despair experienced by the parents of a lost child. But the pain relatives and friends may feel from the loss of a child can also be extreme.

If there is justice on the planet, and if God is all knowing and benevolent, then why does God not stop all evil, all bad events and all disease, for all children and adults? Perhaps when we experience discord and loss, it is a vehicle for us to enable an enhanced appreciation of life. No one can give us a specific, true, unequivocal reason or reasons why bad things happen, or why God permits bad things to occur. But we can try and understand through our own thought process, open mind, and some of the reasons I have given earlier and will continue to give in this book.

"Life is like a dome of many-colored glass,
Stains the white radiance of eternity"

—Percy Bysshe Shelly
August 4, 1792–July 8, 1822
One of the major English Romantic poets

The definition of destiny is a predetermined course of events that will inevitably happen in the future. Did he or she deserve any fate that may have received? Is our fate or destiny predetermined?

If there were no accidents in the universe, would our fate then be predestined? Since there are what appear to be accidents, are the so-called accidents themselves predestined? Are the choices we make already determined? Is our life in the grand scheme of things already completed for us, even though we have free will to choose? Are the choices and decisions we select the choices and decisions that are already predestined? Would this then be free will, if our future were already determined?

It would be free will in a sense, because we did make a choice, even though the choices made were already destined for us. Are the decisions we make choices of our free will that are not predestined? May it be by chance that one's choice is one's destiny? Is then our fate that which we facilitate from our own free will, occur without predetermination?

To understand why bad things happen to good people, we need to ask whether we carve our own destinies or whether they are predestined through synchronicity with the universe. Are there accidents, or is that which occurs part of a grand design? We have the free will to make decisions, but could the decisions we make be those that are predestined? Would this scenario then allow free will? Even though we have free will to make choices, is it free will if those choices are already predestined?

Is all we truly have the present moment? Yes, that is all we have! The present moment is all that exists for us, and it never ages. If we could only remain in the present, how much more vibrant an uninhibited our lives would be. The past is behind us and gone, and the future is ahead and not yet here. With the realization of the importance of the present and its direct implementation and focus in our lives, how different our lives will be.

Are there accidents? Alternatively, is the universe in synchronicity? Is there a divine order to all that is? Can we humans comprehend the non-Newtonian paradigm that in the true reality, nothing causes anything else, but rather, everything is self-existent and is an expression of its own essence?

Chapter 12

Cause and Effect

Ve make choices to drive down a certain street, to take a trip, to change jobs, to get married, to have a child, to have an attitude or not, to be compassionate or not, and on and on and on. What one chooses or what one may not choose will determine that person's destiny, or even someone else's destiny. In our Newtonian reality, everything is about cause and effect, what we may do, and how these choices affect others or us. This is like the domino effect or playing pool: ball A causes ball B to strike ball C.

The combined causal relationship of events and destiny is immeasurable. A better awareness of this relationship would enable more understanding and clarity.

Fate that caused one to experience a tragic loss would also cause a person's grief. What is done is done, and the past cannot be changed. This understanding is not always easily achieved, but yesterday is gone, and we must try to remain in the present.

All problems and causes are relative to the individual's actions and perception. How insignificant my problems seem in relation to world issues and to the physical and mental problems of others. Remember this saying from ancient Persia: *"I cried for not having any shoes until I met a man that had no feet."*

Yet it seems that people's problems are relative to who and where they are. Every set of circumstances, as different as they are, may seem especially relative to one's own situation.

What about the belief we maintain about disappointment, loss, or perhaps a traumatic experience that can be extremely difficult to deal with. Someone with a very strong belief in God could experience the tragic death of a family member and lose faith. This loss of faith could be significant, and regaining it could be difficult. Yet that person should continue to pursue a resolution of some sort, for the sake of continued hope, faith, and understanding. If despair creeps into a person's life, addressing the issue is important, regardless of the type of loss.

It may be beneficial for a period of time to express grief for the loss of a loved one or the loss of a pet, a job, or of some material aspect of one's life. The magnitude of the perception of the loss and one's emotional state should determine the duration of mourning. However, I believe mourning should have certain time limitations.

Note this quotation from Lucius Annaeus Seneca, a Roman philosopher who lived from 4 BC to 65 AD: *Time Heals what Reason Cannot.*

Again, perception of any loss is an important key to triumphing over what is difficult to tolerate and sometimes even to understand. Grief and mourning are important emotions for healing and for limiting anxiety for the individual. How we perceive a given situation is critical for our acceptance. The past is gone and cannot be changed, and it cannot return; therefore, understanding that we must be in the present moment is paramount.

I recall another quotation from John Donne, the early seventeenth–century poet and writer:

"No man is an island, entire of itself…any man's death diminishes me, because I am involved in mankind; and therefore never send to know for whom the bell tolls; it tolls for thee."

Do we truly know how fortunate we are, with the health and material that we do maintain? I suspect that part of the issue is that our recognition of what we are blessed with in our lives should seem more than just relative to us and should not be taken for granted. We need to have a stronger awareness and appreciation of what we possess in our lives, even with a loss that may exist, and to be grateful for what remains, which would ultimately enable greater peace for us.

The more sensitive we are as individuals, the more sensitive we become to the universe, which enables the realization of a greater amount of wisdom, integrity, and peace. One means to obtain this greater sensitivity is to meditate or to become more spiritual or religious. Another means is by engaging in introspective thought, which is not nearly as deep as meditation but is beneficial. This greater sensitivity will ultimately enable to a good degree of relief from the trials, tribulations, and losses in life—not to mention that it will enhance our insight, acceptance, and balance gained. (Please refer to Section 3, Meditation).

There are three categories of events: known causes, probable causes, and unknown causes. An interesting way of looking at cause and effect and why bad things happen is to view destiny working in reverse. A good example of reverse destiny would be the classic movie *It's a Wonderful Life*. James Stewart's character, George Bailey, was granted his wish that he had never been born, and he could then see how the world would have been without him. Obviously, many events were changed. One event involved his saving of his younger brother's life when he was in his early teens and his brother was seven or eight. They were sleigh riding, and his brother fell into a frozen pond and would have drowned if his brother had not been there to save him. His brother went on to become a navy pilot and was responsible for saving a US ship from destruction. In the world where George Bailey had never been born, that same navy ship was sunk, and 475 sailors died because Bailey was not there to save his brother as a child.

Try to imagine the events and life changes that would have occurred because the 475 sailors died, or the life changes that would have occurred because they lived. With the death of the sailors, perhaps four hundred or so marriages did not occur, or many widows were created. Perhaps four hundred or more babies were never born. But if all the sailors lived, a similar but reverse scenario is created. Now we would have 475 survivors with marriages, babies, and families. So many lives would have been affected by this single event, and the effects would have been perpetrated via a chain reaction through the children's children, and so on. Countless generations would have been affected due to the events in the lives of the original sailors.

There are so many changes in either instance, whether the ship sank or it did not. It causes me to stop and think of my actions and my performance in my life—how something I do or do not do that may seem so insignificant may ultimately be very significant. We as individuals cannot be aware of the reverse outcome of our actions. Simply being in a given place or not being there can change so much. I believe this fact really says how important each of our lives is. Every life has extreme importance in the scheme of things; we can all make a difference in some way, whether big or small, by our actions or our inaction.

In another instance from the movie, George Bailey had worked as a delivery boy for an independent pharmacy at age thirteen. The pharmacist had been drinking heavily, and Bailey suspected that a prescription for a sick boy was incorrect, and he did not deliver it. When he returned to the pharmacy, the owner/pharmacist was furious that he did not complete the delivery. But when he showed the pharmacist the prescription, the man fell to his knees in gratitude. But in the existence in which Bailey had not been born, the young boy received the prescription and died, and the pharmacist was ultimately prosecuted.

In a sense, a great gift was given to Bailey in the movie: the ability to see what the world would be like without his presence. What do you suppose the world would be like without our presence as an individual? We very rarely think about how our own actions, as inconsequential as they may seem, can affect someone else or others. An action that seems so insignificant may eventually become very significant. Perhaps simply being present in a given place, with something totally irrelevant going on, can cause a major change. One person's actions may make an incalculable positive or negative contribution, perhaps even to humankind as a whole, yet we may be completely unaware of the magnitude of the change or the difference.

I believe this is evidence of the absolute importance of our actions throughout our lifetimes on the planet. What appears to be an action unrelated to anything important may ultimately be an action with monumental consequences or immeasurable results in the greater scheme of things. Regardless of who we are, our actions as individuals are ultimately significant beyond our knowing or imagination.

Another interesting event relating to cause and effect:

British bacteriologist Alexander Fleming left a pile of experiments in his laboratory for when he returned from his vacation. When he returned, he looked through the stacks of experiments to see which could be salvaged. Most of the experiments had been contaminated. He noticed that one of the experiments had grown mold, and the bacteria it had contained, which was staphylococcus, was gone. This discovery occurred in 1928 and led to the development of penicillin in1944. What would have happened if Fleming had not gone on vacation that year? No penicillin existed, at least until who knows when. Tens of thousands of lives were saved by the discovery, and tens of thousands of lives were affected by the lives that were saved.

Let us now look at another actual event that caused epic and monumental changes on the planet. On August 6 and August 9, 1945, by executive order, President Harry S. Truman ordered the atomic bomb dropped on Hiroshima and Nagasaki in Japan. He believed that this action would end the war, and it did. Within the first two to four months after the bombings, the effects of the bombs killed ninety thousand to one hundred sixty-six thousand people in Hiroshima and sixty thousand to eighty thousand in Nagasaki, with likely half of the deaths in each city occurring on the first day, from the blast and heat generated by the bombs.

As I was writing the above paragraph, I had goose bumps, thinking of the total devastation that occurred. There was the loss of so many lives, and simultaneously the saving of so many lives, due to the war's ending. Can we even begin to imagine the lives lost and the lives changed because of the bomb? Which event, the dropping of or not dropping of the bombs, would have perpetuated the greater change and difference on the planet? In reality, which scenario would have been the most positive? Does the end justify the means? How about the lives saved on both sides due to the war's ending? There were positive and negative actions that did or did not occur because of the deaths. The results and changes that occurred do to the loss of spouses, children, and families. There are also positive and negative acts that will occur because of the lives saved. Think of the new marriages, children, and new, multiple generations. It is difficult or impossible to realize, speculate or know the ultimate outcomes from events that did or did not occur.

Another event of epic proportions was the Cuban Missile Crisis of October 1962, in which the stern but decisive actions of President John F. Kennedy averted and ended what could have been a nuclear war between the United States and what was then the Soviet Union.

We will never know what the results of World War II would have been if the atomic bombs had not been used. How different the planet and life would be today, after multiple generations! The Cuban Missile Crisis was averted, and again, how different the planet might be if it had not been. There are a countless numbers of events through the centuries, which might have appeared either inconsequential or consequential, if we did not know their reverse outcomes.

What truly caused the Japanese to bomb Pearl Harbor, and was that the reason the war started with Japan and the United States? The majority of people would say that the Japanese bombing of Pearl Harbor did start the war with the United States. Would the American part of the world war have occurred if the US Navy had not been at Pearl Harbor? Did it happen because ships and planes were invented? Was it because of the person who invented navigational systems? Was it because the Japanese wanted to dominate the planet? Was there anything the United States could have done to stop the attack and subsequently the war? Was there anything the Japanese government could have done to stop their aggression? Was the war caused by the fact the Japanese people who wanted to start the war were born? Was the bombing of the two Japanese cities the fault of God? Was it President Harry Truman's fault? Was the creation of the bombs the reason the cities were bombed? If the atomic bombs had not been developed, they could not have been deployed. Was it the bomb creators who caused the war, was it the university where they learned their trade as physicists, or was it whatever influenced their desire to become physicists? Was it their parents' fault, because of the environment they were raised in, or their parents' fault for giving birth to them, or their grandparents' fault for giving birth to their parents? All the seemingly incidental events or occurrences mentioned earlier are part of the chain of events and causes, in virtually any event. So, what is the actual cause of anything?

What, in the scope of reality, truly causes anything? What appears to be a cause of an event in most instances is not the sole cause, but it is, rather, the conceptual cause. Paradoxically in the true reality, there is no cause and effect and no duality. Nothing causes anything else; everything is an expression of its own essence and is self-existent. However, life as we know it is not the true reality but is rather a reality based on ego, duality, cause, and effect, and it is influenced by our perception and ego.

Another cause and effect was 9/11 and the attack on the World Trade Center in New York, the subsequent loss of life in Manhattan, and, ultimately, the Afghanistan invasion. If the World Trade Center had not been attacked, there likely would not have been an Afghanistan invasion.

The Cuban Missile Crisis, World War I, World War II, the Korean War, and the Vietnam War, and so many others—were all these horrific events God's fault? I think not. I believe they were human beings' own creation.

God did not cause wars or the dropping of bombs; therefore, God is not responsible for the subsequent deaths that occurred—humanity is. None of us needs to own a company, be a president or a general of a country, or be famous in order to make a positive contribution throughout life. A simple act of generosity or kindness can affect so many lives and actually make difference on the planet because of our actions and subsequent causal relationships.

I believe that we can only speak for ourselves when it comes to what kinds of acts we may or may not have committed, whether we think them good or bad, and what we would consider reprisals assigned to us by God as universe. In reality, we are only aware of our own actions and nobody else's on a daily basis. No one person can actually speak 100 percent truth about anyone's life except for his or her own.

However, I suspect that some people may not be aware of negative acts they committed. Perhaps they were not conscious that what they were doing was wrong. Is ignorance an excuse? Is ignorance the only true crime? Is a negative willful act considered ignorance? If an act is willful and the perpetrator is unaware of the wrongfulness, is ignorance the crime or is the crime the crime in the eyes of God? Both produce the same result. Can ignorance prevail and be excusable, even though we may realize a distinction between right and wrong?

Most people would know that a criminal act such as robbery is wrong and unlawful. The perpetrators of such an act would be guilty of robbery and would undoubtedly have been aware that the act was unlawful. Was this an act in total disregard of law and order, or was it simply done out of ignorance? I suspect that some robbery may be committed in disregard for law and order, because of people's awareness that robbery is unlawful, but in their perception, the robbery in itself might not necessarily have been a wrongful act. Is the commission of wrongful unlawful acts a matter of ignorance in addition to being unlawful? Do we know how God will interpret our acts, or do we even care? I believe, if we search deep enough into our psyche, that we will find the answers needed to explain any penance. Society punishes people who have committed crimes that are designated by the state or federal government as being unlawful. There are different sentences and punishments for different crimes.

However, is there chastisement for people that commit crimes or for unethical or immoral acts that have gone undetected by society but not by God as universe? I believe that justice does exist, if not in this lifetime, then in another.

There is a price that individuals pay for crime, injustice, and immorality. The price, or retribution, is determined by the magnitude of the act. There is an independent but simultaneously dependent mechanism originally initiated by God as universe. This force is an integral part of God as universe, a function that measures the positive and negative acts of individuals. The acts or deeds of individuals emit positive or negative energy, and a part of this energy includes the act's truth, morality, and magnitude, as well as its ultimate evaluation by the universal force. This force emits and returns positive or negative energy to the individual, based upon evaluation of the energy of the individual's good or bad acts.

The energy may enhance a good or positive deed and may project additional positive aspects as rewards to the person, in either material or spiritual forms. The force will also chastise and produce negative effects as warranted, directed back to the individual who emits negative acts. The degree of the reward or chastisement to the individual is determined by the energy and magnitude of the act. Just as objects we hurl into the air always return due to gravity, our positive and negative acts return to us, in positive or negative ways, by the discipline of the universal force. The positive reward or negative discipline is not necessarily instantaneous but will occur eventually. Everything in the universe is interconnected and is part of everything else. In essence, the phrase *"What goes around comes around"* is in fact so, in some form or another.

The existence and description of the reactionary force was derived through my meditation. The existence of the "Reactionary Force," I maintain and believe is an absolute knowing without any doubt. I refer to as God as universe "Reactionary." The "force" directly relates to the truth and morality of the actual judgment of the individuals performance in their life.

Appearance and people's performance can be deceiving at times, and what we view and assume to be true is not necessarily so. It may appear that an individual you know has as an example, great wealth and happiness. The person appears to be happy and to have lots of money, or perhaps appears to be happy without money. Assumption, based on observations alone, is not necessarily fact. Remember that we cannot vouch for anyone's life, happiness, or deeds unless we are with that person on a round-the-clock basis. What appears to be so may not necessarily be that way.

How should we establish and define truth and integrity? Certain acts performed may correlate with simple ignorance. Is our perception that a wrongful act committed by someone is deluded and distorted thinking, or is the wrongful act itself done out of ignorance, independent of perceptual thought? Is true integrity uncontaminated understanding and awareness? Is a wrongful act simply ignorance, or does a misguided perception create the ignorance, which is then sustained simply by being void of evidence? Is ignorance then considered to be a lack of knowledge, or is ignorance a fallacious awareness created by our distorted perception? Does flawed awareness constitute ignorance? If so, what we perceive may then become our interpretation, whether it is true or false. This in turn facilitates how we may view or respond to a given situation. In any event, some negative acts are manifest for that which may be due to our vague and somewhat mixed feelings and to the current insight we then maintain. An enhanced understanding of a subject regarding its truth and its morality will enable a more practical evaluation.

Empirical knowledge is one of the critical ingredients of integrity, followed by truth, which is not necessarily moral, hence the evaluation of the truth. Empirical knowledge, coupled with the evaluation of truth for determination of its morality, equals factual righteousness and subsequently perpetuates integrity. Perceptions can at times influence our evaluation of truth, which may ultimately influence our identification of a subject's morality. Our perception of what is truthful and righteous is not necessarily others interpretations. Assumption and credulity is the archenemy—the nemesis, if you will—of truth and ultimately of morality. We sometimes have an unwillingness or aversion toward researching a subject before formulating an opinion. But the more knowledge we learn about a subject, the more beneficial it will be. Understanding based on factual data will enable a more realistic and enhanced resolution of questions about a subject's morality.

Do some investigation of facts, situations, ideology, and belief systems for your empirical knowledge. As you do so, the truth shall be brought to the surface. As you analyze empirical knowledge, the truth and its morality will determine the factual righteousness of the subject, and ultimately, its integrity.

Integrity Equation:

Empirical knowledge + truth + morality = factual righteousness = INTEGRITY

In a sense, we are judged, and I believe that how we act and perform can determine the quality of the lives that we lead and our ultimate destiny in this life or another. I believe that determination of our ultimate destiny in the afterlife will be measured by the predetermination of our actions during our lives on earth. When the spirit or soul separates from the physical body, it will ascend toward an area or realm of energy that is similar to what the person projected in his or her life on earth. The kind of individuals we were and how we lived our lives on the planet will determine the fate we face in our afterlives. There is in fact a Judgment Day when we leave the planet, in the sense that we will soar to, and remain in, a place that corresponds to the truth, values, and morality we demonstrated in the lives that we maintained on earth. We will remain in either our own heaven, hell, or purgatory for an indefinite period, or at an undetermined time, we will reenter a newborn body on earth for a fresh new life, absolutely unaware of the previous lifetime.

The description of the soul's separation from the body and ascension to the realm described has been proven by kinesiology, a muscle-testing technique described in a book entitled *Muscles: Testing and Function with Posture and Pain* by Kendall and Kendall. John Diamond, MD, the founder of Life-Energy Analysis, uses this muscle-testing technique to determine truth. Diamond's system is also based upon the alternative medical technique of applied kinesiology (AK), founded by George Goodheart, DC. In addition, muscle-testing work for truth is being carried out and studied by David Hawkins, MD, PhD.

[Florence P.] [Kendall]. [*Muscles: Testing and Function with Posture and Pain*]

[Elizabeth K.] [McCreary]

[Patricia G.] [Provance]

[Mary M.] [Rodgers]

[William A.] Romani]

(Lippincott Williams & Wilkins, February 24, 2005)

I have personally experienced the marvel of kinesiology's muscle-testing technique for the truth of current and past events, material objects tested for their positive or negative energy, and for disease diagnosis.

Another aspect of obtaining higher levels of consciousness and which can perpetuate cause and effect responses relates simply being kind as human beings, a different form of energy that pervades many— but not enough—people.

Kindness is contagious, according to a study done by researchers at the University of California, Los Angeles, and the University of Cambridge and the University of Plymouth in the United Kingdom. New research may unlock the mystery. The study is the first of its kind to systematically document this tendency in human nature. It has found that when we see someone helping another person, it gives us a good feeling, which often, in turn, causes us to go out and do something altruistic ourselves.

"Kindness is Contagious, New Study Finds,"

"When you feel this sense of moral 'elevation,' not only do you say you want to be a better person and help others,"

said Simone Schnall of Cambridge, the lead researcher.
"But you actually do when the opportunity presents itself."

"Elevation," a term coined by Thomas Jefferson, is
different from regular happiness, a specific emotion that
we experience only when we see someone else engaged in
virtuous acts, Schnall said.

"Human nature is essentially good," she said. "And
this study proves that seeing good things actually
makes us better."

It is natural for us to seek the positive emotions that
accompany seeing and doing acts of kindness, said
Joseph Ferrari, professor of psychology at DePaul
University. If we saw more positive stories in
the media, it might spur an even greater trend of
compassion, he said.

"If we had people reading about random acts of kindness
it would spread and people would help more people," he
said. "People want to be happy."

I personally believe that positive acts help enable and produce positive events, and negative acts produce a greater number of negative events, hence, positive and negative outcome and replication. Something as simple as a motorist yielding to another vehicle at an intersection can perhaps perpetuate a new thoughtfulness in the person in the vehicle that was yielded to. This simple act of compassion by an individual, maybe never received before by the other motorist, could now become contagious and elevate the other person's awareness or ultimately even his or her level of consciousness in time.

Science in Society Northwestern University Outreach
Initiative: [Shannon] Mehner] *"Kindness is Contagious,*
New Study Finds," April 21, 2010

We may not know what our participation in life may ultimately produce, but we do know the kinds of acts we perform and the awareness we maintain. Realizing the importance of truth and morality in relation to the way we conduct ourselves in life is paramount for others and our own peace of mind. And yes, that ultimately means realizing how our performance may affect our lives and the lives of others, and how it may even possibly affect humankind.

Regardless of the size, cause, and eventual effect of an event, how we react and perform may be as critical as the event itself.

Cause and effect from the very smallest act by one individual can literally change humankind for all time.

SUMMARY OF WHY BAD THINGS HAPPEN

1)   *Are we even supposed to know why bad things happen to adults and children?*

2)   *What we perceive is how we interpret.*

3)   *Our perception is not always the truth.*

4)   *Emotions and perceptions play a key role in how we distinguish and address situations in life.*

5)   *How could we appreciate good without evil? If we did not have bitter, we could not appreciate sweet.*

6)   *If all that exists on the planet is good and pure, could life be appreciated the same way it is now?*

7)   *We are accustomed to polarity and to opposites to enable us to differentiate and then appreciate.*

8)   *Would we ever feel joy without sorrow or pleasure without knowing pain and suffering?*

9)   *Would we be able to appreciate goodness without having a distinguishable comparison of the opposite?*

10) *Is God responsible for all disease and all negativity on the planet?*

11) Do we die in order to appreciate life?

12) Is there a grand design to all that is and all that occurs in the universe?

13) When should God draw the line for the age when children or adults do not get cancer—or any disease, for that matter?

14) Are all acts or events on the planet spontaneous, or are they part of the synchronicity of the design of the divine?

15) The more sensitive we are as individuals, the more sensitive we become to the universe, which enables the attainment of a greater amount of wisdom, integrity, peace, and synchronicity with the universe.

16) Regardless of who we are, the eventual outcome of our actions as individuals is ultimately significant and beyond our knowing or imagination.

17) We do know the kinds of acts we perform and the awareness we maintain.

18) After an event, regardless of the negativity, cause, and eventual effect, how we react and perform may be as critical as the occurrence of the event itself.

SECTION 5

Love

Chapter 13

Romantic Love

With all the various types of love, let's start with romance. Here's a typical dictionary definition of love: "A powerful emotion that manifests itself into deep devotion, affection, and sexual desire."

This may apply to romantic love but may also relate to the following. Love is definitely a powerful emotion. We may have a deep devotion to someone with or without loving that person. We can be devoted to our jobs, to friends, or to other people for many reasons, with or without loving them. We can be affectionate with a person with or without loving him or her. We can even be sexual with some people with or without loving them. There is an obvious, discernible difference between romantic love, the love for others or for material objects, parental and family love, and friends. True romantic love has distinctive dissimilarities with other types of love.

As far as the interpretation of romantic love, there are those people who would say that romantic love is a myth and that it does not exist. It is quite obvious that people who hold this opinion have never experienced true romantic love. Perhaps they have never been in romantic, loving relationships, or possibly unsuccessful relationships have convinced them that romantic love is a myth. For example, some people who think love is a myth might base their opinion on issues they or others have experienced. No doubt, many of their acquaintances have claimed in some way, regarding their relationships that "the honeymoon seems to be over."

How many of you have ever heard of happily married couples, which are likely experiencing true love, needing a marriage counselor for their relationship? How many marriage counselors have in fact seen happily married couples regarding the love in their marriages? It may, then, be safe to speculate that the majority of couples who appear to be in love may actually in fact be in love, and if so, do not require counseling—or perhaps may not be in love and simply do not seek counseling. The exception to this supposition may relate to issues arising from the existence of children from a current or previous marriage that present a problem, or other instances such as stress that may require counseling but which are not directly related to the love the couple has for each other. Therefore, some people who believe that romantic love is a myth have obviously not been in love or met happily married, romantic lovers. One cannot necessarily stereotype certain aspects of human behavior in view of the fact that we are all individuals with diverse experiences and emotions.

Alternatively, therapy may help facilitate saving the marriage of couples with genuine issues. In many instances, therapy can aid in resolving many problems if both parties desire help, are truly honest, and are open to resolution, which ultimately can be brought forth through therapy.

I describe true romantic love as a deep, tender, ineffable feeling of affection and devotion. It's characterized by a mentally and physically electrifying sensation, passion, and intense chemistry toward another person, with whom romance and sex is powerfully desired.

This feeling of romantic love between two people, if real and true, should be continuous and should be sustained unconditionally. Fabricated love and what may appear to be true love but is a fallacious emotion may deteriorate in time.

Romantic love is most different and is not necessarily viewed as a typical emotion; rather, it is a unique state of mind, in a sense, where there are no polarities. Romantic love is a state of mind that enables a powerful but rare sensation to surface toward each other.

In addition, romantic love may not have a semantic opposite like other emotional states of mind. Emotions tend to maintain a semantic opposition, similar to the concepts of good and evil, right and wrong, up and down, and joy and sadness. Unlike typical emotions, romantic love remains a unique state of mind, independent of an opposite or duality. And when we do in fact relate to emotions, they become a means whereby specific emotions perpetuate different behaviors, which remain dependent upon those emotions.

There are other types of love, such as the platonic love we maintain for a sibling, parent, friend, or child, and then there is the love of inanimate objects. All of these are obviously dramatically different from romantic love. Polarities or opposites exist with inanimate objects and within our emotions, but I believe the polarities are absent with romantic love. Romantic love is a realized state of mind, unlike other emotions. Stated from a different perspective, this state of mind is non-dual. Romantic love has no polarities and no duality.

141

I believe that romantic love is an innate, physiological, chemically induced state of mind that remains exceptionally special in comparison with other emotional states. An unusual balance of particular energies between two people triggers the birth of romantic love.

In reality, the "chemistry" generally described by people at the beginning of relationships does in fact exist, and it facilitates the attraction, cultivation, and potential of imminent romantic love. The initial chemical attraction is not necessarily sexual, although sex is desirable. Rather, this attraction is a general, unique personal and character appeal that goes beyond the sexual aspect and enables the chemical reaction to surface.

There is an ecstatic, blissful feeling that we may experience at the beginning of a relationship. True, love if real should be sustainable and should not diminish in a month or two—or ever. Again, I believe we either love or we do not love; loving another for a period of time and then not loving is not possible, nor is loving a little or loving a great deal possible in a relationship. There is no "I loved him or her for a year or so" or "I loved him or her a little or a lot." Again, and I cannot emphasize this enough, you either love or you do not love; we cannot love for a given period and then not love. That is not how romantic love works!

True love is unconditional and everlasting and it cannot cease.

Romantic Love cannot grow and it cannot diminish; it simply is, and it simply shall be. If you love a person truly, it is not possible to stop loving. What can grow in a true loving relationship, or diminish in a fallacious relationship, are emotions like sensitivity, compassion, and empathy. There would be a greater understanding and devotion of the partners, as they become confidants and romantic lovers, and then the simple aspect of just becoming better friends. You begin to experience trust, affection, satisfaction, contentment, and joy with the other person. These are the attributes that begin to develop in the true, loving relationship.

There will be no hours or days of punishment, anger, or abuse, and no days without talking to the other. There is no personified ego; if you truly love the other person, neither of you will permit a dispute to survive. In true love, each will make the necessary sacrifices for the other because of the love for the other. If you truly love the other, you will not permit discord to continue. I believe this logic, when realized, becomes unmistakably evident.

The actual sensation may be described by some as ineffable, or incapable of being put into words. Yet you will experience a dramatic desire and an innate, absolute knowing of true romantic love and euphoria far beyond classic infatuation. You know without any doubt, without any hint of reservation, that this is real, true romantic love. It is not necessary to ask yourself the question, "Do I truly love her or him?" The question is not necessary, because you already know the answer. You know for sure that this is true romantic love. In true love, the "honeymoon" will not end; rather, it will be sustained forever. The uniqueness and newness will obviously begin to fade, but not the love itself.

Unlike romantic love, other types of love have duality. For instance, one might love one make of car and hate another, and perhaps one even loves or hates his or her boss, or I really dislike my wife's friend, or I really dislike my husband's friend. One does not actually love or hate the car or boss or friend in the same sense one maintains romantic love for another person, hence the distinction.

Only romantic love emanates without any polarities; romantic love simply exists on the same continuum of "love," without opposites or duality. There are those who would insist that "love" and "not love" present a dualistic set of terms; however, "not love" is not an opposite to love, but rather is a term that exists on the same continuum. Therefore, unlike other emotions, romantic love exhibits an absence of an opposite connotation. Furthermore, in reality, "love" and "not love" do not denote opposites, because of the absence of a distinguishable word for comparison. Romantic love in itself exists as an independent sensation or structure of awareness, and it remains non-dual, unalterable, and irreversible.

To reiterate, with regard to one's feelings, one cannot love a person and then not love or even hate the same person unless what one experienced was not romantic love to begin with. "I loved him or her at one time, but not anymore." This is not possible. I believe that if a person feels and believes that she or he loves another, and then at a later time, believes that he or she does not, then it was not love at the outset. We cannot love, then not love, and then conceivably feel we even hate the same person. We love or we do not love. It is actually that simple. However, such simplicity is not always that easily achieved or understood, unless true romantic love is present.

Chapter 14

Flawed Relationships

True love should not be confused with what I term as fallacious "Desperate Ecstasy" that sometimes facilitates a so-called loving relationship that is actually flawed. "Desperate Ecstasy" is enabled through one's own desperate desire to be involved with another. This infatuation period usually begins to diminish within weeks or months, with the unaccepted realization that this feeling was not the romantic love the person initially believed it was. In such instances, we often have the tendency to delude ourselves into believing that it cannot be so, and we continue with our relationship while attempting to convince ourselves that the relationship is truly loving and viable. This type of erroneous romantic love is in fact an egoist intervention for the benefit and satisfaction of personal and selfish needs. One facet of this intervention might be a state of codependency, which can play an enormous role in fallacious affairs and can enable extended continuance for longer durations. Other facets may involve satisfaction of selfish personal needs such as sex, financial security, companionship, and the fulfillment of other emotional needs.

Extensions of flawed relationships require significantly more effort to maintain the alleged romantic love. The fact that the relationship is not true love is not usually apparent to the parties involved. They typically delude themselves into actually believing that the relationship involves genuine love in order to pacify and satisfy ego and conscience. Denying that they have made a mistake also allows them to retain a certain level of self-esteem and perhaps avoid the hassle of searching for another relationship.

If a couple needs to work quite often at their relationship, then I do not believe it was a proper relationship from the beginning. Unfortunately, most people do not realize that a couple with the presence of true love should not require much, if any, effort in order for their relationship to be successful and to flourish. I believe that if true love exists for each other, this will automatically enable a thriving relationship, with virtually no obstacles. If true love is present, whatever disputes or disruptions may transpire will be resolved rather quickly.

However, effort—perhaps significant effort—is likely required if the couple does not have true romantic love for the other. The awareness and evidence of this becomes obvious when obstacles in the marriage or relationship began to occur. True romantic love is unconditional; there is no "I have to do this" or "I have to do that." It is not necessary for either person to change his or her ways to meet the demands of the other for the love to flourish when it is true love. Preconditions in the relationship will not be necessary when true love exists. If preconditions are thought to be necessary by one or the other, then one should reassess the actual validity of the relationship.

On occasion, couples remain together for various reasons not associated with love but rather with a comfort level from simply being in a relationship. Remaining together for other reasons—because of a child, for example, or because of financial needs and individual personal and emotional requirements—would necessitate some effort and, at times, substantial attempts to preserve and sustain the relationship. So I am not suggesting that preserving the relationship or marriage shouldn't be undertaken, but rather or not to do so should be determined by the individuals involved.

At times, the feelings of one person in the relationship may have changed dramatically; to such a degree that he or she simply does not want to continue in the relationship. At this juncture in the relationship, the people involved should exert the most significant effort to determine their true feelings toward each other, without reservation, ambivalence, or delusion in finding the truth. The awareness of a flawed relationship should have been determined in the beginning, but sometimes the infatuation and euphoria that occurs early on obscures the ability to distinguish the truth. However, at this point, the truth is critical if the people wish for the relationship to continue and to be caring and amicable. The truth may be a painful but a necessary realization for the ultimate benefit of all concerned.

If the people wish to continue, they must initiate significant effort in identifying, addressing, and rectifying the issues that exist in order to preserve the relationship. If the couple cannot accomplish this together, then therapy through counseling may be considered. Both people should be in full agreement about solving issues for the salvation of the relationship. If agreeing to seek therapy is not mutual, then that disagreement in itself could be the deal breaker.

When do people decide that their relationship should not continue? What instances, what reasons, what events might have occurred that would lead us to believe we no longer want to be involved in a relationship? Is it simply that our feelings toward our spouses or partners have changed? At what point should we determine the degree of effort it would require to save the relationship, and when do we decide that it is too far-gone or that we simply don't care anymore? Should we remain together for the sake of our children, or because we would be lonely without the other, or for financial reasons, for security, or perhaps for companionship and sexual needs. On the other hand, are some of the previous invalid reasons for forming a relationship part of the reason we are together to begin with and are just maintaining a delusion of actual romantic love? Is there another man or woman we now care about, which negates any of the other reasons?

We should ask ourselves whether our needs are significant enough for us to remain together. Do we now realize we are not in love? Or do we feel we are still in love? Have we ever been in love? Do we want to spend the rest of our lives in this relationship? Will the partners feel better and be better off without the other person? Can the people live alone for a time without being lonely?

What can change in a relationship be confused with a change in love. If love truly existed in the beginning, then it will not change. What changes is not an alteration in love. Changes involve, in the beginning of a lack of understanding or a new awareness about the other individual as the two begin living together. These individual changes now realized about the other person involve such things as moods, habits, perceptions, attitudes, and communication, all of which may be confused with a change in or a loss of love. One or both people at this time in the relationship may not fulfill the others needs. Moreover, a person may become angry, cynical, sarcastic, or jealous. The love itself if real would not have presented these new issues. However, the reality of living together may have altered the people's feelings and perceptions about each other. The relationship may begin to evoke discontentment and arguments, and the people may become easily frustrated.

Love is and should be unconditional and sustainable. Whenever disputes transpire and obstacles surface, if true love is present, they should be capable of being resolved rapidly without further ado. If any of the earlier negative issues exist in the beginning of the relationship, the people involved should take a hard look at the viability of the relationship.

Regarding the importance of a timeout between our relationships, having space or alone time is critical. I refer to both singular and plural as relationships because there are those who may have been in another relationship, perhaps before the current one, or immediately after the present one. Concurrent relationships may be construed as being one ongoing relationship because of all the dependencies mentioned earlier: that the person cannot be alone or that the person stays with the partner for financial reasons, for security, for companionship, and for satisfying sexual desires.

Recognizable, true love without delusion involves knowing that without reservation, the individual is the person that you wish to be with the rest of your life. It means recognizing that person, unequivocally and unconditionally, as the love of your life, with no uncertainties whatsoever. In fact, this scenario and the search for true love may result in the necessity of the searcher to be alone in life, rather than settling for less than he or she truly longs for and wants in a relationship. But true romantic love, although rare, does exist. It is my belief that fulfillment simply depends on who we are, what we are prepared to accept, and how long we are willing to wait. Do we want true love, no love, or settling for less? The first step is to develop an understanding of yourself; be honest with yourself about relationships, without delusions. This will enable you to keep from settling for less, and you will be able to live and be alone without being lonely.

Remember that if the feeling of love changes for one partner or the other, I do not believe it was mutual true love to begin with. The relationship initially was likely an infatuation that evolved to a stage that one or both people thought was love. Perhaps one of them deluded himself or herself for one of these reasons: companionship, security, financial independence, loneliness, great sex, "my friends are all married," or "I must marry before no one wants me because I am too old." Furthermore, the partners may not have a desire to deal with the dating or bar scene again, and therefore, they remain in the erroneous relationship. Settling, for whatever reason, is only a means of justifying the continued existence of the flawed relationship.

We may remain in the relationship for some of the reasons mentioned earlier. Or we may not recognize our true feelings or may settle for less than we desire and need in the relationship because it is just okay or perhaps comfortable. Instinctively, we may refuse to recognize our true feelings in order to enable the relationship to continue. A bizarre satisfaction may be realized from the selfish material or emotional comforts obtained in a relationship. Settling for less may bring an undesirable end to what we had thought would be everlasting.

How many times I settled for less than I desired in a romantic relationship, for some of the selfish reasons I have mentioned! I believe that most of the time, we know if this is true love and if this is "the one" that we have been searching for. But we delude ourselves deliberately, for selfish reasons that we refuse to admit to ourselves, and prolong the relationship, knowing in our heart it is not correct—but it is comfortable and satisfies our immediate personal needs.

I finally made up my mind several years ago that I was not going to settle for less than I wanted in a relationship any longer. I had been in so many relationships for the wrong reasons. If I had to describe why I was in a relationship that I knew was wrong for so long, it was because of loneliness. I did not like the feeling of not being in a relationship, being alone and forced into the singles circuit. I did not like living alone or being at home without someone in my life; it made me very uncomfortable. Perhaps my loneliness was partially due to a codependency issue. However, the person I was with needed to meet certain criteria. The person had to be attractive, and I had to feel a certain amount of appeal and engage in good interaction. Even though I knew this was not sufficient, it did meet my immediate personal needs. But I decided that if searching for and not finding the right person meant that I would never marry or live with someone, then so be it. I would continue to date, but not for very long if I knew the person I was currently dating was not "the one."

After being divorced for over twenty years, I did meet a woman in 2007: my wife, Pam. Pam was the one I had been searching for, she was it, and she was the one. God granted my prayer to find someone to love and to love me in return. Finally realizing and rectifying my codependency issue enabled my undiluted, true feelings to surface and be recognized. In addition, I had a better understanding of myself through introspective thought, thereby eliminating the usual deluded and ambivalent feelings that might occur in the beginning of a relationship, generating fallacious "Desperate Ecstasy." Being the true romantic that I am and still to be fortunate enough to find the love of my life was a true blessing.

Chapter 15

Types of Love and Fear

There are different types of love: the romantic love of another, the love of a parent, a child, a sibling, a relative, and a friend—not to mention the love we maintain for ourselves. All of this is love, but with a variance of emotion that depends on which category of love we are addressing.

It is essential to understand the love of oneself before we can truly comprehend a sincere romantic love of another. Do we love who we are, what we say, how we act, and what we think? Are we happy with ourselves? Can we be alone without being lonely? Understanding and resolving these questions is essential and, furthermore, fundamental before we can realistically extend true love to another. Without a resolution of these questions, we only enable fallacious "Desperate Ecstasy" to surface in a relationship.

It is paramount to recognize and comprehend our own possible issues and to rectify the negative emotions before we achieve true understanding and realization and can extend our love to others. The lack of love for oneself or the absence of romantic love toward another individual may be responsible for discontentment, which can breed frustration, fury, and perhaps destruction from some people. These problems may continue to disrupt both the other person's life and perhaps one's own until one finds the internal and external love needed for a joyful, peaceful existence. Love of oneself and for another person, as well as a love of God, is indispensable for a joyful life that will ultimately achieve happiness and contentment. To have love of oneself may automatically enable peace and joy to surface.

To love oneself is first to understand oneself. This is what the Buddha teaches for knowledge and understanding. We need to recognize and understand our true feelings about different aspects of life, not deluding ourselves about what is true or not. We must recognize that some feelings and emotions we maintain may be egocentric. Moreover, what we tell someone else regarding any situation or about how we feel about them romantically, may simply be gain for our own pleasure and satisfaction. What we express to the other person about our relationship if not sincere, ultimately will be emotionally hurtful.

Whether one is dealing with a companion, coworker, parent, sibling, or relative, or perhaps is contemplating a potential romantic affair, a person may not recognize his or her true feelings because of sometimes unrecognized selfishness and the desire to satisfy one's own personal needs. Perhaps deluding oneself with a statement that one wants to believe is true is meant to pacify the conscience in the hope of eliminating one's own guilt. Should one agree with the statement of another, even though one truly does not believe it, in order to gain acceptance? Sometimes insecurity can breed delusional feelings about a person or situation or enable deliberate ambivalence to surface. This in turn induces one to say and do things that are not his or her true feelings or beliefs. One tries to convince oneself that they are true because he or she wants them to be so to enable the relationship to continue.

We sometimes settle for less than we desire in relationships, knowing deep down in the bottom of our hearts that this is not what we really want. However, we may continue with the relationships if it is okay or just comfortable. Attempting to be void of guilt and to circumvent having to continue the search for another may be some of the reasons the so-called loving relationship continues. Deluded feelings and emotions can be so easily generated to enable relationships to continue. But with true understanding and knowing, our true selves can preclude the typical delusions and deliberate ambivalence from surfacing.

Love in any category, but especially romantic love, is powerful. But romantic love is a unique emotion, which, if true, will be sustained and will not diminish.

What happens, though, if one recognizes romantic love for a person, but the love one offers is not accepted even though it is true love? Sometimes the fear of being hurt and rejected by the other perpetuates an emotional barrier, and false reasons may be projected, that would justify contamination of the relationship to keep it from ever being consummated. What an incredible loss this would be, to forego what may be romantic love, because of one's fear of being hurt! Perhaps the person has previously been emotionally hurt, and this fear remains. Or this fear may simply exist, whether or not a previous loss has been suffered. In any event, if this fear exists, obviously it may inhibit one's ability to facilitate a potential true, loving relationship in one's life.

The following quotations about love may depict the bitterness of loss and the ineffable bliss of ecstasy.

Alfred Lord Tennyson (August 6, 1809–October 6, 1892) was Poet Laureate of the United Kingdom during much of Queen Victoria's reign.

I hold it true, whate'er befall;
I feel it, when I sorrow most;
'Tis better to have loved and lost
Than never to have loved at all.

J. Krishnamurti (May 11, 1895–February 17, 1986) was an Indian writer and speaker on philosophical and spiritual subjects.

The moment you have in your heart this extraordinary thing called love and feel the depth, the delight, the ecstasy of it, you will discover that for you the world is transformed.

Aristotle (384 BC–322 BC) was a Greek philosopher and polymath, a student of Plato, and a teacher of Alexander the Great.

Love is composed of a single soul inhabiting two bodies.

John Lennon (October 9, 1940–December 8, 1980) was an English musician and singer-songwriter who rose to worldwide fame.

All you need is love.

Hafiz (1320–1389) was a beautiful, mystic Sufi poet from Persia.

All I know is love, and I find my heart infinite and everywhere.

Khalil Gibran (1883–1930) was a Lebanese poet.

All these things shall love do unto you that you may know the secrets of your heart, and in that knowledge become a fragment of Life's heart.

Rumi (September 30, 1207–December 17, 1273) was a Persian poet and philosopher who participated in a literary renaissance.

Only love itself can explain love and lovers.

I recall a personal experience with a woman named Kelly. Kelly and I had been seeing each other for about two months. It was late one evening, and we had just returned to her home from dinner. We were sitting on her sofa and were beginning to embrace each other, but after a few minutes, she began to cry profusely. I asked what was wrong. She did not reply at first but finally stated that she was upset because she could not be hurt again. Further explanation revealed that this feeling was due to an experience she had had with her previous husband. Apparently, another woman was involved. Her discovery of the other woman's existence ultimately led to divorce and subsequently, I suspect, to her fear of being hurt again.

Fear of failure is the culprit in various aspects of life, including our not following our hearts' desire. Whether we had a passion for a profession that we did not pursue because of the fear of failure, or whether we did not continue with a potential romantic love in fear of being hurt—both are related to the fear of loss.

If you are fortunate enough to have true love appear, do not permit it to escape; rather, seize it. You will know absolute true love when it appears, without the delusion of infatuation or fallacious "Desperate Ecstasy." You will know if the person is the one for whom you have been searching. We do have an absolute knowing regarding romantic love. Do not permit your ego's fear of loss to dictate your decision. Every person has a degree of romanticism that he or she should permit to dominate the decision, rather than allowing undesirable fear to embrace and eradicate what may very well have been the pinnacle of happiness in the person's life. It is important to remember that there are three things in life money cannot buy: love, peace, and joy. If one is fortunate to experience true love, there may never be another opportunity for it to arise. Do not permit love to slip away; find the courage and the time to love. I do not believe that there is anything truly worthwhile remembering without love.

"Carpe diem" is a phrase from a Latin poem by Horace, the leading Roman lyric poet at the time of Augustus. It means, "seize the day," and it continues with "putting as little trust as possible in the future." I conclude with, seize the love opportunity.

A related phrase that depicts the present in Hebrew: אם לא עכשיו, אימתי

This means, "And if not now, when?" (Pirkei Avoth 1:14)

Summary of Romantic Love

1)   Romantic love is a unique awareness that enables a powerful but rare sensation to surface.

2)   Romantic love is a realized state of mind unlike other emotions and inanimate objects or platonic relationships.

3)   An unusual balance of particular energies between two people triggers the birth of romantic love.

4)   The initial attraction is not sexual, although sex is desirable. Rather, it is a general, personal, physical, and character appeal beyond the sexual aspect that enables a chemical reaction of energy between two people to surface.

5)   The actual sensation may be described as ineffable, and one will experience a dramatic desire for the other, recognizably beyond classic infatuation, with an innate absolute knowing without any doubt of "true romantic love."

6)   It is not necessary for either person to attach conditional demands on the other for the love to flourish when it is true love.

7)   We must recognize our honest, unselfish, true feelings without enabling delusions to surface in a relationship before we can truly comprehend sincere romantic love of another.

   a)   It is essential to understand the love of oneself before extending our love to another.

   b)   Do we love who we are, what we say, how we act, and what we think?

159

c) *Can we live alone without being lonely?*

d) *Are we happy with ourselves? We must recognize and comprehend our own possible issues.*

e) *If possible, we must rectify any negative emotions we may retain.*

f) *It is critical and fundamental to differentiate between "desperate ecstasy" and true love.*

In true love, one has no reservations. True love is unquestionable, indisputable, and totally recognizable.

SECTION 6

Time

Chapter 16

Awareness of Truth

The quality and purpose of life does not diminish as we grow older. Generally speaking, one's value as an individual, to others and oneself, and the importance of life remain unchanged or may increase with time. The value and appreciation of life appears to become more precious with age; I suspect this is due to the limited time a person may have remaining on the planet. Like many other material or nonmaterial aspects of life, when something becomes less plentiful, it seems to hold more value

The realization of our impermanence is something we all recognize, but what is lacking is taking that understanding of the importance and urgency and putting it into action. We need to recognize how we perceive, perform, and utilize our uncontaminated, true feelings regarding our destinies early on in our lives' paths. We may choose not to recognize this important truth even though we actually know it, due to our unwillingness to face certain unpleasant issues at that particular time. These are issues, we are reluctant to address and tend to delay until a later time for various reasons that we then justify as legitimate. But issues that we permit to linger will actually corrupt our thinking and attitudes and will circumvent any action and fulfillment we may have gained. Yet we have a tendency to proceed on a fallacious path because at the time it seems the easier road to follow. But remember that procrastination and taking no action is action in itself. Dietrich Bonhoeffer, a German pastor and theologian and an organizer of resistance against the Nazis, stated, *"Not to act is to act," "Not to speak is to speak,"* and *"Absence in the face of evil is itself evil."*

Through positive action, and living out the once-evaded truth about who we are, we will usually appreciate our values more. This in turn enhances our innate consciousness and empirical wisdom, and it will foster, to some degree, an open-mindedness toward others and toward the universe as God. For each of us to find our own peace, and open-mindedness is critical. Understanding rather than judging is one of the key elements of peace. When we can try to understand why an act has transpired, rather than applying judgment to it, we will then be on the path to inner peace.

All moments in time are of equal importance; however, as mentioned earlier, moments in later years seem to have an even greater significance than those that occurred earlier, for many individuals. Some people treasure moments because they are aware of the limited time they have remaining on the planet. Some of us may begin to ponder what is truly important in life. As with so many aspects of life, generally when we possess an abundance of something, we seem to value it less. Acquiring riches and material possessions often merely create comfort but also unease in us, so fearful are we of losing them. Some of us may live in constant fear of loss of almost anything. However, and happily, the idea of losing the non-material aspects of life need spark no such concern. Perhaps though one places a lesser emphasis on one's life expectancy when young, and may not yet feel the need to focus on what is truly important in life. But if a significant lack of something is felt, one may then begin to place a greater emphasis on it.

Hence, older people may place a greater emphasis on life and hold it to be much more precious.

In previous periods of our lives, deceptive, deluded thought may have circumvented the truth about ourselves and about who we are, what we truly desire, and what is important in our lives. Our deluded thought may also have corrupted others. Much flawed thought sometimes relates to the material aspects of life, with too much emphasis on wealth and excessive thoughts of prestige or power. Certainly, material and particular emotional aspects of life should be given some consideration, but they are not the prerequisites for peace and happiness. What era of life we find ourselves in dictates what we consider important and relevant at that time. The past and future do not hold nearly the same importance as the present. However, previous periods in our lives did maintain equal or conceivably even greater importance at that stage, but the significance the past once had may now be secondary in the present.

However, there is a fundamental need to expand the spectrum of understanding of one's purpose, and that one needs investigative measurers that can help determine the truth about who one is and about one's ultimate desires and destiny. One should not judge one's own importance in life simply by the present, even though the present currently has the most relevance and substance. What was important to us at an earlier time in life obviously may not have the same meaning and importance now. Therefore, what may seem significant now, in the present, may not hold the same importance in the future.

As the Persian poet Rumi said, *"To be one with the truth for just a moment, is worth more than the world and life itself."*

This awareness about ourselves is why it is essential for us to understand, without erroneous deluded thought, which stems from our own self-centered desires, or perhaps someone else's desires for us.

It's preferable that we understand what is truly important for us early on, but we still need to understand these things in later stages of life. What should be our inspiration? What should we embrace? What would be most enduring? Imagination is powerful, but it can be positive and negative. What we imagine can actually become valued and precious to our decisions and to our souls. So it's important to have a vision of one's true desires in the future, vision comes from the Latin "To See." Meditation provides an excellent quiet time to learn about oneself. In addition to learn what is truly important not only now, but in the future. Meditation can aid in the determination of an action plan and how individuals relate to our ideas and to themselves. Our emotions and perceptions determine our attitudes and ultimately our choices, hence our ability and freedom to choose. Being truly honest with ourselves, and recognizing our true feelings without egoist manifestations, will help to bring us the understanding needed.

The recognition and discipline needed to recognize the truth may be more easily enabled through meditation if self-contemplation is not beneficial. (Please refer to section 3 on meditation.) Success in recognizing our true feelings will only bring us true happiness and will help us realize life's purpose and meaning. At some point in all our lives, we recognize that material possessions alone give us comfort but do not necessarily create happiness or peace. We must also recognize the truth in what we believe about our personal relationships. What importance do we assign to our daily job and activities? Is what we do and how we perform daily our truth, and is it righteous? Is what we do daily what we desire? All of these things—personal relationships, our jobs, our daily activities, and our daily performance—facilitate either happiness or discontentment. Nevertheless, true happiness and peace do not exist in brief or passing moments, but rather in a *constant* and enduring state of mind.

We must decide how we truly view our lives at this period. Are we truly happy, or have we deluded ourselves into thinking we are, to enable our ego and consciousness satisfaction. Will we permit ourselves to recognize our true feelings, or are we reluctant to permit the truth to surface? If we do not already know the truth about ourselves, with proper focus, we can actually recognize how we truly feel inside without seeking help from others. However, if this knowledge is not available through our own efforts, then we should consider professional help to learn the truth.

If we finally decide to identify and recognize the truth about ourselves and take action to facilitate it, this will be truly a monumental step. Once we understand that we can realize and recognize the truth, if we do not take corrective action, we will only prolong our discontent.

When some of us express ourselves to others on certain subjects, we sometimes often do not necessarily tell the truth. We have a tendency not to permit others to know the truth about what we truly believe unless the others believe as we do. If we feel that others do not feel or believe the same as we do and therefore will not accept us, we often have a propensity to conceal the truth. We must attempt to be individual thinkers without the influence of concerns about others. Individuality will only enhance our lives and enable us to find peace without submitting to the will of others. Recognizing our true feelings regarding life, our purpose, and our destiny as early as possible can be extremely beneficial, and can dramatically augment our existence. However, recognition of the truth at any age will make life more beneficial and meaningful. What we do as individuals is truly important for us in our lives, rather than how others think we should perform, or accomplish.

Time can play a role in our happiness. The longer it takes us to recognize truth and rectify erroneous situations and beliefs in our lives the longer it will take to find our purpose. Sometimes we deliberately delay actions that would enable a release from flawed daily situations or relationships. We engage in pleasurable, more easily achieved activities rather than addressing the more difficult problems at their inception. But, it is more beneficial to engage in the more difficult tasks at the outset, even though they may not be desirable.

When you complete unpleasant tasks first, there is then a greater appreciation of your desires through delayed gratification. An individual daily may attend to his or her easiest activities first. However, doing this would make for a very discouraging day when you know that the toughest part of your day is still ahead. Would it not be better to complete the difficult work first and save the best for last? This would enable a better appreciation of your day. You would then look forward to the rest of your day rather than being wary of it.

Delayed gratification can relate to so much more in life. I remember as a child wanting to eat the crust of my peanut butter and jelly sandwich first to save the best part, the center, for last. You might go to a movie theater and try to find a candy that lasts the longest rather than buying the one you like the best. Try to realize situations that would improve with delayed gratification. Applying delayed gratification to as many aspects of life as possible will only improve our general attitudes and perceptions, and we will ultimately gain more pleasure and efficiency in our daily lives. In addition, if we address the more difficult issues at the outset, we will gain more peace and appreciation *throughout the day, throughout the years, and even throughout our lives*. This applies to any aspect of our daily activities that is not necessarily desirable and that we have a tendency to delay. If something must be done, don't do it later—do it now.

Chapter 17

Plateaus of Life

It is fascinating to think about different stages in one's life. I can remember my first day of school when I was five. I was excited to go to school for the first time. My mother was concerned about me walking to school with just other friends, and she had my older cousin walk me to school. I remember that he hung my coat in the cloakroom for me. But after several days, my kindergarten teacher called my mother to ask that my cousin permit me to hang my own coat. What was important to me at that time in my life was playing with toys and other kids, hanging my own coat, and eventually tying my own shoes.

What was important at age five would not have the same meaning or importance at ten, twenty, or thirty years of age. Yet, whatever age we currently are, certain things are of the greatest importance, relevance, and meaning to us at that particular plateau. The present maintains the greatest importance for us. One who is thirty years old would likely have different desires than those of a person who is fifty years old, and each would probably view the other's desires as less significant than his or her own. What each of us considers important is relative to our age and to our particular time of life. Our desires change, sometimes dramatically, at different stages of life. Things we were adamant about in our earlier lives, how we functioned and perceived, and what we enjoyed, we may look at from a completely different point of view at a later stage.

What was important, say, at age twenty or thirty may be secondary now, or we may have no interest at all at whatever it was, even looking back at age forty or fifty. Yet whatever age we are, at that time in our life, that respective age seems to transcend the utmost significance for that period. We can reflect on how we appreciate and give so much relevance to things of our current age and might wonder how we perceived our lives so differently when we were younger. We now perceive life in other ways at an older age. Every different age plateau has so much meaning and implication for each respective time in our lives. Reflections about earlier years in our lives, other than as learning experiences, now seem less significant compared with the present.

Sometimes an older person may view a younger person's life as more mundane and less significant than his or her own when aspects of the younger life seem so elementary. I suspect that this is because an older person has "been there and done that." Meanwhile, older people's lives may be viewed in a similar way by younger people; the older people's desires and lives may seem not at all desirable to the younger. Younger people may believe that older people do not realize that "times are different" and that the older generation "just does not understand." What the younger people do not recognize is that the changes are primarily technological, with the advent of things like fax machines, the Internet, e-mail, cell phones, advanced designs of automobiles, organic foods, and work-from-home jobs. Life itself remains the same. People continue to live in homes, although they might be different from homes of the past; work; drive cars; eat three meals a day; and have fun. Life remains unchanged, with the exception of scientific advancements in society.

Some people might say the technological changes have affected our lives in different respects and have created a different pace for life. However, life, purpose, and meaning remain unchanged. Love, peace, and joy continue to be desirable. People continue to seek knowledge, wealth, and power. Life has not changed; it is one's perception of life that changes, due to peoples altered perception of events of our reality, sometimes obscured by the advanced pace of society.

Many young people may regard older people in certain negative ways: older people cannot move as quickly, they are not necessarily as active, their memory is not as good, and they spend their time watching TV, playing cards, or lying around. Perhaps they are considered old-fashioned by the younger set. Some younger people also believe that older people's ideas may not be relevant to the age we live in.

If one is retired and is not as productive in society, no longer contributing in the workforce, others may view the person as no longer having significance. After all, the person has no direct involvement in society. However, it never ceases to amaze me that some of the younger people who hold these beliefs somehow have dramatic changes of heart about who and what are significant if they themselves are fortunate enough to attain old age. These conclusions by some younger people probably correspond with their perceptions of their current stages in life.

Yet, each group, the younger and the older, finds its own stage of life significant, pertinent, and meaningful with respect to that age. The older age group may believe that a good percentage of the younger age group is not nearly as wise about life, without the older taking into consideration the academic achievements of the younger people, and that a good percentage of the younger maintain a belief that is not bias regarding the older generation. In addition, many of the younger people may have made significant achievement regarding an advanced understanding and perception of their lives, purpose and meaning that some of the older people could fined as a learning experience. By comparison, a good percentage of the older may usually maintain a higher degree of awareness regarding empirical knowledge and a certain degree of wisdom, which possibly would come to some people with older age but is more related to sensitivity to the universe, including a higher consciousness.

Life is all relative to where one is at a given time in one's life. Understanding what is truly important can be difficult. Where one is in terms of a level of consciousness can determine the degree of wisdom one has gained or realized at a given period in life. I believe there is a distinct dichotomy between intelligence and wisdom. Intelligence is the ability to learn, which includes what one may have achieved academically. However, wisdom is the comprehension of what is true or right coupled with one's ability to optimally apply perception, knowledge, judgment, and discernment. Wisdom itself as mentioned earlier, unfortunately is not guaranteed with age but is realized through one's sensitivity to humanity and to the universe. This means that there is also a good percentage of the younger set that does maintain a higher degree of wisdom, likely due to a self-observed mind coupled with a higher level of innate consciousness.

I have always admired and loved the way Carl Jung describes the stages in life through archetypes. These are characterized in four types. The first and lowest is the *athlete*, which signifies the time in our adult lives when things are about the body—how it looks and what it does. Our bodies are the means by which we can be identified. But as we mature, we move into the archetype of the *warrior*. The warrior signifies the time in our lives when importance is placed on how much we can earn, when we will make our first million and how many things we can acquire. This involves thoughts such as who we can compete against, who we can defeat, and who we are better than. The third archetype is the *statesman* or *stateswoman*, which signifies the time in our lives when we begin to have more of an interest in serving than in wanting to know what is in it for us. The fourth is the archetype of the *spirit*, where we begin to understand what it means to be in this world but not of this world.

Some of us may be fortunate enough to become aware of the specific plateaus that Carl Jung describes and what is truly important about our existence at those junctures, and perhaps with even our own variation of Jung's description. Based on my own understanding of my life, I suspect I am a classic example of Jung's descriptions, and I now find myself in the spirit stage.

When we wake up one morning and suddenly realize we are thirty, forty, fifty, sixty, or older do we think about our accomplishments in our lives including our children and family? Do we ask whether we should have done this with our lives or should have done that? Do we wonder if we are now too old to do this or that? What do we think about, and what are our thoughts? Do we even ask ourselves these questions? Are we very happy with our lives at the current juncture? Do we reflect on other options we should have followed yet did not? Is it too late to change? Do we even care?

Are we physically, mentally and financially capable of doing what we now regret we did not accomplish at an earlier time? If we feel we are capable, then we should consider the pursuit, especially if we have the financial independence to so. Are we as individuals willing to relinquish material possessions and engage in a change in lifestyle if it is necessary to facilitate our desires? With passion, we will achieve our goals of whatever we have constantly desired but never pursued. If our passion is substantial enough, we should develop the drive to do so. Achieving our hearts' desire will facilitate fulfillment in our lives and will fill the void we may have carried for such a prolonged period.

We often do not realize how short a time we have on earth, and we often overlook the value of sensitivity, understanding, compassion, and less judgementalism. Yet extending these values toward others is a considerable contributor in actually finding our own peace. But we often delude ourselves about what is truly important and sometimes act selfishly and inconsiderately. Are we satisfied with our contributions to others and to ourselves? When we leave the planet, will we have been happy with our lives and how we have lived? Would it not be a dreadful thought to be on one's deathbed and not have "played one's own music?" Imagine never accomplishing or even trying the things we have thought about and wanted to do with dedication and passion!

I was reflecting with my daughter about how time has passed so quickly. I returned to St. Louis from Florida in 1992. That was twenty years ago, and it truly seems like the last month or two. Being sixty-seven years old, I think that if God grants me health and life for another twenty years or so, how fortunate I will be. At eighty-seven, how will I feel about my life, and how will I view the life that remains? For that matter, how do I feel about my life today, and how do I feel about the life that remains? If I have aspirations about goals for the next twenty years, what are they? Did I have goals for the past twenty years? If I had goals, did I achieve them? Am I satisfied with my life at my current age? I had similar reflections in my twenties about how it seemed like only yesterday that I was in high school, and the same thing happened in college and then in my late twenties. In my thirties, forties, and fifties, on occasions I also reflected on how fast time seemed to be passing. I find it somewhat discouraging but interesting, looking back in hindsight and summarizing what I should have done or not done.

Will we ever learn enough from previous periods in our lives to understand and utilize the empirical knowledge gained to benefit us in the present or the future? Or will we instead just make the same mistakes again? Will we wait until later to take action, hoping that it is not too late? Perhaps by then, another ten or twenty years will have elapsed. Then there will be the stark realization that those twenty years have gone by and that we have not accomplished what we wanted. In addition, we may say to ourselves, "I cannot believe another ten or twenty years has passed; it seems like yesterday that this or that happened. On the other hand, I wish I had done this or that differently or not at all. However, I cannot believe I have not started this project as yet, and ten or twenty years have passed again." Does any of this have any significance to our lives? Should we care? Do we care? Should we continue to procrastinate and delay that which may be the true happiness we have longed for, or should we take action now?

Yes, time has a way of slipping away. If we could only realize this before those ten or twenty years pass and the time for achieving our ultimate goals expires! And this phenomenon is different from the delayed gratification previously mentioned. The necessities for the achievement of our ultimate goal have initial actions to be taken, some of which may have been distasteful, hence the procrastination and ultimate delay.

I love to paint in oils; as mentioned earlier, I always felt I was participating in my purpose in life when I was painting, and it truly gives me the most pleasure. And most of all, I continue to have the sense that it is extremely important that I paint; I must contribute and leave something behind from my life, something that is a definitive accomplishment rather than a personal achievement or monetary gain. I suspect I believed that oil painting was permanent, material, and significant and appreciated by my family, friends, and others. It just seemed to me that I needed to leave more of a contribution from my life than simply the definition of being a good person. I believe my paintings satisfy this need and desire, as of kind of a contribution of a material permanence of myself that I could leave behind.

A couple of years ago, I felt the desire to write this book. I felt it was important for me to accomplish what I realize now was a lengthy and arduous task. I believed that through my self-awareness, I would be contributing to others in helping them to realize a better understanding and appreciation of their lives and existence. So I felt I might contribute to others and perhaps even make a difference on the planet by this another means. Some people would say, "Do you know how difficult it is to write and publish a successful book?" However, I told my family and others that upon completion of the book, if my work made a positive difference in only one life, then the book would have been worthwhile.

Think of individuals who have made a difference in their lives and perhaps a difference in ours, individuals from the past two thousand years or so. All of those people from history have changed so many lives and made such a positive difference by their actions and personal contributions.

The Great Rabbi of Loubavitch said, *"Even in the darkest place, the light of a single candle can be seen far and wide."*

The Talmud, the Jewish sacred text of oral law and tradition, states, *"Save one life and you save the world."* May we as humans be motivated and inspired to contribute and comprehend the power of one individual's actions to make a difference on the planet. All of us have the power to make a difference in some fashion; it is a matter of focus, determination, and taking action.

There is a lack of love, peace, and joy in so many lives, as people often show insensitivity toward others. It is sometimes inconceivable how; some people treat others with such a lack of consideration or understanding! If we could only be more sympathetic about the reasons why others behave as they do, we might become significantly less judgmental.

Think of the idea that people are not isolated from one other but that all humankind is interconnected. Or think of the stunning awareness that death is part of life and that we are all born to die. This is part of our mutual existence, our life.

Chapter 18

Time Is Passing Faster

With regard to our ages, how do we discern time itself as a measurement? What is time besides a measurement? We know that one day has twenty-four hours, one hour has sixty minutes, and one minute has sixty seconds. These are measurements denoted by humans, originally based on the earth's revolution around the sun. Egyptian astronomers had one of the first methods to divide days into equal parts, using devices like sundials, shadow clocks, and merkhet plumb lines.

Can time actually pass more quickly, as we sometimes feel that it does? Or do we have that perception just because our lives are busier? Time does seem to pass more quickly when we are busy than when we are not. However, it does not explain why people who are not busy also find that time is passing rather quickly. There are theories that this state of mind is psychological; some younger people who are not as busy believe time is passing more slowly while some older people believe it is passing more quickly. Another theory relates these feelings about time to our ages, as percentages of our lifetimes; we feel that time is passing more quickly as we grow older because the percentage of time we have left is less. A biological theory maintains that the speeding of time is associated with metabolic changes in our bodies, causing us to feel that time passes more quickly as we grow older. I do not believe that our imaginations or psychological or metabolic changes in our bodies make time pass more quickly; they only aid in making us feel that it does.

We might think that being busy with jobs or projects is the reason time seems to pass more quickly. One reason might be that when we were children, time seemed much slower because we had nothing specific to do. When we are older, our days seem to be more prearranged and we have specific tasks. When we are busy, it appears that time passes much more quickly. This may be true to a certain extent. However, I am basically retired and writing a book at home at my leisure. There are no urgent needs, and there is nothing specific to do, and yet time is roaring by very quickly. The years seem like months, the months like weeks, and the weeks as if it is "Monday and then suddenly the weekend."

I have done a significant amount of research with different age groups about how quickly time is passing. I find that the majority, about 90 percent, also feel that time is moving very quickly—much more quickly than it seems like it should. This consensus is in age groups from high school to the late seventies.

Einstein's work abundantly and amazingly showed that time is relative. In 1907, his general theory of relativity showed that clocks run more quickly at higher altitudes because they experience a weaker gravitational force than clocks on the surface of the earth. The phenomenon, called gravitational time dilation, was demonstrated by installing atomic clocks on jets and flying them at high altitudes. Just as

Einstein predicted, clocks flown at an altitude of thirty thousand feet ran faster than those left behind on the earth's surface. Gravitational time dilation is also noticed in global positioning satellites, which need to have their clocks regularly adjusted due to the time differential.

This phenomenon also means that your upper torso ages more quickly than your lower and that people living on the top floor of a tall building age more quickly than those on the first floor. Time passes more slowly for people living at sea level than it does for those at higher altitudes. The difference is extremely small, but it does exist.

Many parts of the universe expand at the speed of light in all directions, and, perhaps more unexpectedly, some of the galaxies we can see right now through the Hubble telescope are currently moving away from us more quickly than the speed of light. Subatomic particles may have been traveling faster that the speed of light scientists announced—or was it an error? This description is based on the Hubble term "constant" in relation to the expansion of the universe. The Hubble telescope is one of the tools currently used to obtain information that enables scientists to measure the expansion of the universe and its speed.

In Einstein's theory of relativity, when a twin in a spaceship travels at a very high speed, close to the speed of light for a length of time and travels independently of the movement of universe, then upon returning to earth, that twin would be much younger than the twin who remained on earth.

[Ker] [Than] *"Particles Moved Faster Than The Speed of Light?"* (National Geographic News, September 23, 2011)

I have always had an unusual fascination with time, space, and the universe. I am not an astrophysicist, and therefore should not have a cosmological theory, but in the course of researching time, space, and the speed of light, I actually had an epiphany. I believe that because the earth is in fact moving at the same speed as the universe, parts of which is expanding at the speed of light and greater, that time would be increasing in speed rather than slowing down or remaining constant. This would be due to the earth and the universe moving together at almost the same speed rather than moving independently of each other. Einstein's theory accepts that time would slow down if a spaceship were to approach the speed of light. The narrative of mine is simply based on my epiphany, nothing else. Conversely, because parts of the universe are expanding at the speed of light and faster, its expansion together with the earth's movement within the universe's movement, and with the universe's speed of light causes the earth to enter an altered and different altitude and position subsequently increasing times speed. It has been proven by scientists that time passes more quickly in clocks at high altitudes and in jet planes and in satellites circling the earth. Just as passengers within a commercial aircraft are moving at the planes speed of five hundred miles per hour, because of speed of the aircraft, so is the earth moving within the universe at its very high speed. I believe time would then be truly passing more quickly for us on earth when one applies Einstein's theory of relativity.

[Dave] [Rothstein] [*"Is the Universe Expanding Faster Than the Speed of light"*?] Ask the Astronomer, Astronomy Department at Cornell University, September 2003 http://curious.astro.cornell.edu/question.php? number=575

Applying Einstein's theory of time dilation in a variation, now having two of the same relative constants, the earth and the universe moving together at a speed, close to or greater than the speed of light, would then cause time to increase in speed opposed to slowing down, or remaining a constant and unchanged.

The earth and the universe are moving together rather than independently of each other. The earth is constantly changing position. It remains in the same relative position with respect to the surroundings in our solar system, galaxy, and beyond, but changes its overall placement. Although the earth is not quite in the same position in relation to the other planets, the overall expansion of the universe has caused a change. It is like dough with blueberries in the oven: the blueberries represent galaxies, the dough represents space, when the dough begins to rise, the blueberries change distance in relation to the other blueberries because of the expansion of the dough. In the same manner, the planets and stars do change positions as the universe expands.

I believe time actually is passing more quickly on earth for all age groups. In addition, time is constantly increasing in speed as the universe continues to expand and increase in speed.

An interesting comparison regarding the speed at which time passes and our age: if some of us live to the ripe old age of ninety-plus years, we will have slept away a third of our lifetimes. Sleeping an average of eight hours in a twenty-four hour day at ninety-plus years old means, we will have actually slept about thirty years of our lives.

Do not take time for granted; it is extremely important to cherish every precious moment. Utilize your time wisely.

SUMMARY OF PLATEAUS OF LIFE

1) *Life appears to become more valued and appreciated with age. Material or nonmaterial aspects of life become more precious with time and increase in value.*

2) *We all recognize our impermanent existence, but what is lacking is taking immediate action upon our awareness.*

3) *Identification and recognition of our true feelings as soon as possible is essential.*

4) *Procrastination and taking no action is action in itself.*

5) *With the implementation of positive actions, our values and their importance will increase and in turn will enhance our innate consciousness.*

6) *It is important to understand rather than judge.*

7) *Deceptive, deluded thought circumvents the truth about ourselves. Do not put too much emphasis on the material and not enough on true purpose.*

8) *One should not judge one's own importance in life by simply the present. It is necessary to expand one's spectrum of understanding of one's purpose and find ways to determine the truth and eliminate erroneous, deluded thought.*

9) *It is important to have a vision of one's true desires in the future.*

10) *Our emotions and perceptions determine our attitudes and ultimately our choices. We must recognize that material things alone give us comfort but not necessarily happiness and certainly not peace.*

11) *Is what we do daily that which we desire? Are we reluctant and apprehensive about permitting the truth to surface?*

12) *We must attempt to be individual thinkers without the influence of others or concern about their acceptance.*

13) *It can take time to recognize truth and rectify erroneous situations. There is a greater appreciation of one's desires through delayed gratification, after undesirable tasks are completed first.*

14) *What we hold important seems to be relative to our age and the particular time in our life; that which is important now is not always significant later in life.*

15) *Learn the truth of who we are and our ultimate desires and destiny.*

16) *It is fundamental for us to understand ourselves without fallacious deluded thoughts and to fulfill our own desires and no one else's.*

17) *Meditation can aid in the determination of an action plan and how individuals relate to our ideas and to us.*

18) *Recognition of our true feelings will facilitate for us true happiness and the importance and the realization of life's purpose and meaning.*

19) True happiness exists as a sustained state of mind. Individuality will only enhance our life and enable us to find true peace.

20) We must address the more difficult issues in our activities at the outset to gain more peace and appreciation. Our desires change, sometimes dramatically, at different stages of life and with time. Each age plateau has its own meanings and implications.

21) Life itself remains unchanged; it is one's perception of life that changes. With passion, we will achieve whatever we desire. Sensitivity, understanding, compassion, and open-mindedness are major contributors in finding peace.

22) Are we satisfied with our contributions to others and to ourselves? When we leave the planet, will we have been truly happy with our life and how we have lived?

23) Have we learned enough in our life to understand and utilize the empirical knowledge gained to benefit us in the present and the future?

24) People from history have changed so many lives and made such a positive difference by their actions and personal contributions to others and to humankind.

SECTION 7

Energy

Chapter 19

Being in the Present

Many different types of energy exist on the planet. The six most basic forms of energy are kinetic, potential, thermal, chemical, electromagnetic, and nuclear. There are also many different cultures on the planet that recognize a different type of energy and that understand and utilize the energy of life for healing. This is a type of energy known as universal energy.

Prana, Num, Roohah, Lung Ki, Chi—many different cultures have their own energy healing methods. Universal energy is much more effective when it is attuned through the body's chakra system, which is a tremendous healing process. I have personally been a student and a teacher of universal energy, and if used properly, it is indeed an extremely effective method for healing virtually any disease. In conventional medicine, early detection of most diseases is most important for treatment, it is helpful but is not necessarily essential with the use of universal energy. Nevertheless, if I may briefly describe universal energy, it is not the body or human energy described by some religious groups; rather, it is energy that one directs from the universe. The mind actually coordinates the energy, directing and focusing it to its destination. The energy does not flow through the healer's body but rather is directed by the healer's mind to the patient.

The chakra system must be opened in order to do so effectively. Chakras are seven major points or centers of spiritual energy in our bodies where universal energy is transferred. The seven chakras are crown, third eye, throat, heart, solar plexus, sacral, and root. It is important to learn the locations and uses of each chakra and the techniques for transferring universal energy. There are many groups that practice the use of universal energy for healing. Universal energy is extremely effective for healing in virtually any problem. Without going into any specific detail, I would suggest that you conduct your own investigation of universal energy in your own city.

Another form of energy is applied kinesiology AK, as mentioned earlier in the book. It is a means by which a diagnosis is made by using muscle testing as a mechanism to examine how a person's body is functioning. AK uses a method referred to as manual muscle testing. The system of AK indicates that every organ dysfunction is accompanied by a weakness in a specific corresponding muscle. Finding a weak muscle enables the practitioner to pinpoint illness in the corresponding internal organs.

With the AK technique, a patient stands with his or her left arm fully extended, perpendicular to the body. The examiner then touches the patient's top wrist area while the patient touches another part of his or her body with the other hand. If the minimal pressure applied to the wrist causes the arm to go weak and drop, that is an indication of an issue involving the part of the body that the patient is touching with the other hand. But if the arm remains firm and does not drop, the touched area is normal. The examiner can also apply this technique to determine truth when making a statement or touching an object. The truth of the statement is determined in the same manner, in which having the arm remain extended and strong signifies that the statement is true, and having the arm go weak suggests that the statement is false. This does not apply to one asking questions, only making direct statements in the testing process. This method can be utilized to learn truth from the present and the past. I personally have experienced AK, and it is effective, accurate, and actually astounding.

Unlike other forms of energy, in general, the natural energy that we project in our everyday life can attract positive or negative natural energy from others. The emission of energy from others can affect one's own demeanor if he or she permits it to do so. Both types of energy can and do affect our lives in different ways. For example, in many instances all of us have experienced either positive or negative energy from ourselves or other people. A bad attitude accompanied by negative energy from an individual can affect us dramatically. Attitude or depression can be contagious if we are not cognizant of our states of mind. We may escape from a reality of discomfort, but we escape to a dramatically different and damaging reality of depression. It is important to be aware of the causes of depression to determine the type of treatment and to use as personal alerts to help us avoid episodes of depression or nip them in the bud before they become an issue.

Events that have occurred in the past that one recalls as unconstructive or negative memories should be addressed in a positive, productive manner. The energy we expend on negative events of the past and the present is wasted and may create negative emotions in our everyday lives. The negative events may inhibit our ability to function in our own normality. We have the ability to maintain and focus enough energy to facilitate change in our lives and to repudiate the involuntary emergence of the memory of negative events. Why do these negative thoughts reoccur, and can we avoid or eliminate them?

So much has been written over past centuries about living in the present moment. If we could only live in the present moment, how different life would be! Living in the present moment is paramount for a healthier, more constructive, and positive lifestyle. Living in the present moment is, in fact, the only true reality. Events of the past do not exist in our present reality except as a reflection. The present is where we are, hence the importance of being in our actual physical reality. The past does not exist any longer, and the future is not here yet.

If the past does not survive, except in our minds, why do we so often reflect on negative events of months or years gone by that cannot be changed? Why do we often torment ourselves, looking back to negative events? Have you ever found yourself looking to the past and reliving an incident repeatedly? Perhaps I should have said this to him or her, or perhaps I should have said that. If I would have said whatever then, I would feel better now. Alternatively, I really should have said or done this or that.

Reliving and rehashing negative events is not beneficial to one's peace of mind and demeanor in the present. The only time one should reflect on the past is if that reflection is going to be a positive and beneficial contribution to the present or perhaps to the future. It is futile to reflect on the past for anything other than positive reasons, and doing so may create negative emotions or despair. The intensity of a negative thought or scenario increases when it is repeated in the mind. The past cannot change, but reflecting upon it can be a learning experience that enables constructive results in the present or aids us in guidance for the future. Though we do not always do so, we should learn from mistakes that were made. We have a tendency to repeat them, so there are techniques to strengthen and reinforce our ability to avoid negative aspects of the past and the future.

We often mull over something that we do not wish to occur because we are worried that it will. Then the chances of it occurring actually increase dramatically. (Please refer to Section 3 on Meditation regarding manifesting and reoccurrences.) The same aspect applies to the reoccurrence of unwanted memories. Some people seem to derive a bizarre satisfaction in reliving negative occurrences of the past. I suspect that this satisfaction comes from our attempts to determine the correctness of our behavior in the past situations. Perhaps we also seek reassurance that we acted correctly in the past circumstances.

But either way, we may find ourselves constantly reliving a given situation. We may think about what he or she said then, or what they did, to you or to someone else, last month or last year or at some other time. We might think about what she, he, or we said or did in a past situation and perhaps what others or we should have done differently. But whatever happened in the past cannot change in the present. For one to dwell on the same negative thoughts or events is futile. Furthermore, the thoughts or events can create frustration, which in turn can be responsible for irritability, which can breed anxiety and ultimately depression.

Have you ever recalled a situation that was distasteful and said to yourself, "I am not going to think about this any longer" or "I will not permit this situation to disturb me ever again?" You may have attempted to divert your attention by picking up a book, watching television, or striking up a conversation with someone. The following technique is similar, but it is a rather more structured and focused process to facilitate successful reduction or elimination of unwanted thoughts of the past or concerns of the future.

Rather than contemplating the thought repeatedly, simply recognize whatever it is, and let it go. Sometimes this is more easily said than done, but I have found tremendous success in a method that I term the "Cognitive Diversionary Thought Process," or DTP. The following technique is a method for reducing and eliminating negative thoughts: just letting them go. Let the thought go, even if it caused issues. This does not apply to something recent that has been reoccurring and may still be part of your life—a situation that you do not wish to think about because it may ultimately produce more negative thoughts and perhaps irritability and despair but unfortunately is ongoing. The negative situations I refer to are those of the past, which cannot be changed.

Realize that there is no advantage in recalling those negative situations unless the recollection is going to have a beneficial, positive aspect for you in the present. The same would apply to situations that may relate to the future. Reduction and even elimination of negative thoughts may be accomplished through the cognitive DTP. "I am not going to think about those negative situations anymore!"

This letting go is not always easily achieved; we cannot stop the initial thought, but we can reduce and eventually eliminate its repetition through the DTP. Diversion can be positive at times as a means to a successful end. We may divert a body of water to prevent a flood or to increase the depth of a channel. We may divert the attention of someone to avoid an incident. In a military exercise, we may divert the attention of the enemy to gain the upper hand in an assault. Diversion can be positive, hence the Diversionary Thought Process. In beginning this process, the initial negative thought will appear, and then we can begin the DTP. Remember the common example of telling someone not to think about a pink elephant; the first thought in the person's head is of a pink elephant. But after the initial unwanted thought, we do have the ability to focus cognitively and immediately and to divert our attention elsewhere.

We must first understand and *accept* that the constant repetition of the same negative thought is not going to change whatever occurred in the past that plagues us. Utilization of our energy on the same negative thought creates unnecessary and unwanted emotions, which may ultimately lead to negative states of mind. To avoid and eventually conquer the unwanted thoughts, when they occur, immediately start thinking about something else, relative to where you are. If you are at work, start to find something in your work to take your interest away from the unwanted thought. Pick up the phone and call someone. If you can take a short break, go for a walk. Soak yourself in positive thought before you return to work. If you do return and continue to have difficulty, go online to find something business-related or something else. If it is not possible to go online for personal pleasure, then go online with something related to your work. Talk to someone at work about a work problem.

If you are at home, apply the same techniques for whatever relates to you or your family. In the car, apply similar techniques. If someone is with you in the car, start talking about another subject. If alone in the car, you can still think of something else important that is positive. Perhaps turn on the radio to a talk show or to some music you like. Intense focus and commitment is key to overcoming the negativity.

I always had a fear of flying, especially just before and during takeoff. What really helped me was picking up a magazine or striking up a conversation with the person sitting next to me. However, before

I was able to accomplish this, I would take one or two Valium. They helped me relax and moved me from a nervous state to a more normal state for the flight. I would be awake and alert. Depending upon the length of the flight, when we landed, I was totally relaxed through the landing, and then I could potentially fall asleep from the drug, needing to have several cups of strong coffee and to sit in the airport terminal for a while before I could proceed. I certainly do not recommend any drug but rather, again, focus and commitment to the process.

You may have done something similar to the DTP technique before but without focused structure and direction. Apply intense focus, which is key to the diversion you have selected, to facilitate the conquest of the memory of the negative thoughts. The repetition of diversionary thoughts is like striking a blow to something. With enough blows and with properly directed force, your opponent—in this instance, the negative thought—eventually loses the battle, and you win.

Apply the previous techniques in an appropriate way when an unwanted thought enters your mind. Or think of the most pleasurable, positive instance that has ever occurred in your life. Use this to divert your thought process and prevent the negativity from entering your mind again. Continue this technique daily, if necessary, until you are able to stop the unwanted thoughts without continuing to utilize the DTP. You eventually will forget what you did not want to remember to begin with—the negative thought.

One instance I use for one of my pleasurable diversions occurred when I lived on the west coast of Florida. It was a gorgeous day, about 11:00 a.m. and 82 degrees, with sunshine, a bright blue sky, and a few stark white Cumulus clouds. The water of the Gulf of Mexico was an exquisite green-blue in color, with the wind at about ten to twelve knots and the seas about one half foot to a foot. It was a perfect day to be under sail and to be alive. Even today, when I think about that time on the water, I become so tranquil, so uninhibited, so peaceful, and so in that moment.

You can actually start to build resistance and immunity to most unwanted thoughts. The more you utilize the DTP, the stronger your resistance becomes to the unwanted thoughts. Positive thinking, intense focus, and the will for success are paramount and are the ingredients of achievement. We must recognize and eliminate the bizarre satisfaction we may get from remembering and dwelling on these unwanted thoughts.

I suspect the repetition of a negative thought stems from the reliving of the situation and changing in your mind what actually occurred or perhaps thinking of a better way you should have dealt with the situation. However, you cannot change the past; it is behind us forever and remains unalterable. This reflection may momentarily cause you to feel better, but not for long. There is no constructive purpose deliberately recalling and dwelling on negative thoughts. Negative thoughts can occur without your summoning them, but you can stop the repetition. You will be amazed how, with practice, this technique can change your life. It will ultimately inhibit and eventually may eliminate the unwanted thoughts or memories. Do you recall how some people say that if a lie is told enough, for a long enough period of time, we began to believe the lie? In the same way, if we create enough diversion, with repetition, when the negative thought appears, we can eventually reduce its recurrence. In this way, we can conceivably and ultimately enable a huge reduction or elimination of the thought, thereby alleviating any ensuing unhappiness or irritability. In addition, we will have less stress in our lives. This technique can be applied to virtually any negative recollection that perpetuates stress, irritability, or anxiety. With practice and time, you start to build resistance to the unconstructive thoughts reoccurring or, at the very least, have the frequency of the thoughts reduced and dissipate more quickly.

Apply the DTP technique directly to any negative thought or anxiety as soon as it appears, in the same manner described earlier or later in the summary. Proper directed focus with DTP may also inhibit the development of potential negative chemical imbalances in the brain, which can be catalysts in perpetuating anxiety and depression. If at the outset you recognize and successfully address irritability, sometimes the precursor of anxiety, this will usually not permit the manifestation of the anxiety to develop. In the beginning of utilizing the DTP, be focused and persistent; try not to become distracted or frustrated. There may be occasions when it seems difficult to focus on the diversion, but as with most techniques or any learning process, in time you will eventually gain more ease in implementing the process effectively.

I recall another instance from about fifteen years ago. I had become very depressed, and I had called my internist for an antidepressant. At the time, it did not occur to me that I probably should have contacted a therapist. The antidepressant was Prozac; I do not recall the milligrams. After several days, not only was I not feeling better, but I felt like I was going to jump out of my skin. I called the doctor, and he said that everything was okay and that it would take longer for the drug to become effective. I do not think he realized the extent of the condition I was trying to describe. After a few more days without any relief from the "jumping out of my skin" feeling or the depression, I decided to stop the Prozac myself.

Within about three or four days, the majority of the nervous symptoms subsided, and for whatever reason, I did not feel nearly as depressed. I believe that what actually happened was that I was so relieved from the horrible nervous feeling of the side effects of the drug that almost all of the depression was now gone. The remainder of the depression completely dissipated after about a week or so with no medication. One might say that the Prozac, which caused the horrible feeling of nervousness, was actually the facilitator of a "diversion" that ultimately perpetuated my release from depression. So even a side effect from medication can be an unintentional solution to an issue. I say "solution," but the root cause of the issue was not determined. I certainly do not maintain that side effects are beneficial, and I would not attempt to induce them, but this instance does demonstrate how they were effective for me.

However, I would not recommend permitting oneself to be engulfed in depression before taking action; you should contact a physician or a therapist. However, you may with the first sign of irritability, initiate the DTP. Do not dwell on the thoughts that are causing your irritability; this will only enhance the problem. Imagine and utilize this process in the same manner in which you would recognize and treat a cold. At the first sign of a cold, you likely would first begin to take vitamin C or consume juice, soup, and lots of fluid to slow the cold's progress and inhibit it from becoming full-blown. You are nipping the cold in the bud; the DTP can serve the same purpose to keep unwanted thoughts from evolving and becoming issues. Calling your physician should always be your first option for any medical or psychological problem. However, if the DTP is applied at the very beginning of what you believe is the start of an issue for you, and it is not working for you after a couple of days and you feel perhaps as though your condition is staying the same or worsening, then seek appropriate medical attention immediately. And I do not recommend the use of the DTP technique if you are already in a state of depression. However, if you are being treated, and even if you are on medication, the DTP may supplement and enhance your recovery, with the approval of your physician.

Nip stress, irritability, or anxiety in the bud. With positive energy, focused properly, you will avoid having to deal with the possible irritability or anxiety that may be occurring in your life. What I describe earlier can be accomplished with practice and patience. As with anything else in life, you will find that the more you practice the cognitive technique, the more rapidly the results will begin to appear. It worked for others and me, and it can work for you, too.

Marcus Aurelius (121–180 AD) was a Roman emperor and was considered one of the most important Stoic philosophers. Stoics presented their philosophy as a way of life, and they thought that the best indication of an individual's philosophy was not what a person said but how he or she behaved. Aurelius's central philosophical opinions are similar to the teachings of Epictetus (55–135 AD). Both men emphasized that inner freedom is to be achieved through submission to providence and from detachment from everything not in our power.

Non-detachment can relate to negative thoughts from the past and to concerns for the future. Future events have not occurred; therefore, it is not beneficial to dwell on instances that may have completely different outcomes than what are imagined, especially if the outcome you imagine is negative. Any future situations or concerns should be addressed with the implementation of the necessary appropriate preparations needed that would aid in your future's outcome. Then detach yourself from the future outcome. It is extremely important to *understand* that it is beyond your power and ability to do anything further regarding the future and its outcome. It is imperative to detach ourselves from the outcome of that over which we have no control.

Consider this excerpt from "The Rubaiyat" by the tenth-century Persian philosopher and poet Omar Khayyam:

The Moving Finger writes; and having writ Moves on; nor all your piety and wit shall lure it back to cancel half a line nor all your tears wash out a word of it...

In other words...

The moving finger writes and moves on to the next words in the line of script, and all the wisdom and joking cannot change what was or what has occurred in life. In addition, all our tears can't change a word of what has occurred. The past is behind us, and we must be in the present moment.

SUMMARY OF DIVERSIONARY
THOUGHT PROCESS

1)   Recognize whatever it is, and let it go.

2)   Be positive; do not permit a negative thought to survive.

3)   There is no positive purpose or reason for negative thoughts, unless it is for your benefit in the present or future.

4)   Understand that the constant repetition of the same negative thought is not going to change whatever occurred in the past or the concerns of the present or future.

5)   Detach yourself from the outcome of the future.

6)   Start thinking about a diversion that is relative to and appropriate for where you are.

7)   Apply intense focus to the diversion you selected to facilitate conquest over the negative thoughts.

8)   If the thought should reoccur, repeat the process again and continue as long as necessary. (Focus)

9)   Alternatively, in addition to the aforementioned, think of the most pleasurable, positive instance that has ever occurred in your life.

10) With focus and relentless determination and the realization of the futility in dwelling on negative thoughts, you will achieve your goals.

Chapter 20

Receiving Energy

I believe that another form of energy is the energy that is actually emitted from genius.

I must share with you an experience that occurred at the St. Louis Art Museum in about 2001. It was at an exhibition of the Artists of the Petit Boulevard, featuring many of the French Impressionists for a limited engagement. In the course of the exhibit, I viewed the self-portrait of van Gogh and had the most peculiar sensation. It felt almost as though I was being drawn into the painting, and my eyes locked onto the piece of work. I felt as if I were mesmerized, and I could not stop gazing. It was very difficult to focus on anything else. As much as I wanted to turn away, it was extremely arduous, because it felt so good. With much dismay and focus, I was able to remove myself from the experience. I thought to myself, "What has happened to me; what captured me?" I had experienced a most unusual and uncanny sensation.

I saw another work, by Seurat, on a huge canvas: *A Sunday Afternoon on the Island of La Grande Jatte*. I began to view the painting, and it was truly a magnificent canvas. My eyes were locked again on the painting. I experienced a feeling of almost euphoria, with intense goose bumps all over my body and an almost simultaneous sense of peace and joy. I became emotional, and tears began to run down my cheeks. It was truly as though I could feel an energy of the brilliance from the painting—energy that perhaps transported me to a place of the pure essence of the artist's work, I later believed. It was almost as though I could somehow feel the pure genius of the artist. I tried to hide my tears from the friends I was with but then felt it was not necessary to do so. Perhaps I was experiencing this event because of my interest in art and because of the fact that I do paint. In addition, perhaps my open mind and sensitivity paved the way to the awesome experience.

I believe that if we encompass a certain degree of sensitivity to the universe, with an open, self-observed mind, we may occasionally experience different types of energy. One of those is that of genius, or simply a higher level of positive energy, regardless of the relationship of the subject or entity. One's sensitivity, an open mind, and the belief that anything is possible can enable awareness of genius. These experiences all occurred spontaneously, and I had had no previous hint or slightest thought regarding the occurrences.

Perhaps at a different level, not nearly as intense as the experience at the art museum but certainly as profound, is music, which can also move me incredibly. The music I refer to is mostly classical in nature, but in particular, I'm thinking of certain Puccini arias. A couple of the classics are Richard Wagner's *Lohengrin*: "Prelude to Act 3" and Wagner's "Overture" to *Tannhauser*. In the "Overture," there is a passage predominately featuring strings and brass. Both are very strong. The trombones seem to be competing with the strings, but in reality, they are very synchronized and truly complement each other. From the genius of Wagner in this particular passage of this piece, I can become emotional at different times and feel awe-inspired and stimulated almost to a euphoric state of mind. I occasionally rewind and listen to the passage repeatedly for the incredible pleasure I gain. For those of you who know this piece and the passage I refer to, you know what I am referencing. For those of you who do not know *Tannhauser*, if you can appreciate classical music and listen to this selection, you will know what part I am indicating.

Another selection I love and can become emotional with is Bach's "Air on a G String." And, of course, "Ava Maria." I suspect that it is the genius of the compositions that I must somehow identify with, which is my only explanation for how I feel. The music itself becomes an emotional, joyful experience for me. In addition, how much I love Puccini and especially his arias, in particular, "Recondita armonia" (*Tosca*), "Che gelida manina" (*la Bohème*), and "Nessun dorma" (*Tosca*). I cannot understand a word sung, but somehow I am able to feel the meaning and the intensity and appreciate the wonder of the arias unbelievable inspirational and emotional presentation, with such awesome beauty and genius.

Another phenomenon that has occurred many times when I've visited the St. Louis Botanical Garden was and unique form of energy in itself. In this one particular place in the garden, and that is a bench that seats three or four people. The total area is approximately fifteen by forty feet, encompassed within an open wooden framework, and flanked from the inside with shrubs and flowers. The framework at either end of this space includes at the center a wooden circle.

The ceiling is framed with wooden slats and interwoven with green foliage but is open enough for the sky to be barely visible. The area's facade blocks the majority of direct sunlight throughout the day. Behind the area is a fountain, and in the front beyond the wooden perimeter is a walking path to other areas of the garden. The path is close enough that you can see people walking, but sitting on the bench, you are not easily viewed by others through the greenery.

Invariably, when I walk into this area, I experience a shower of energy. The best way to describe the type of energy would be as a very low-voltage surge of electricity throughout my body. The energy is subtle enough, but quite obvious and sustained; not uncomfortable, but rather pleasurable and relaxing. On each occasion, the energy in the beginning is strong, but it diminishes gradually as I remain in this space; even before I leave the area, I can only feel very small amounts of energy. I did not know if there was a meaning to what was occurring then, or if it in fact had a meaning.

Once, I visited the area with a friend, with whom I had studied universal energy. During that study period, we had had our seven chakras opened by our teacher at that time, Master Luong Minh Dang. My very good friend Paymon reminded me that the master had stated that when we walked into an area with departed but lost souls or souls that had not yet been released from their earthly domain, the energy from our immediate presence facilitated their release to the light or guided them to their spiritual path. Hence, the strong energy in the beginning when entering the area and virtually none when leaving.

On another occasion, my wife and I were attending our friend's son's wedding. The experience occurred in the middle of the ceremony. We were seated, and suddenly, I was overcome with the most extraordinary surge of energy. The type of energy, which

Master Luong Minh Dang on occasion would transfer to us. I could not understand why I was experiencing this energy, but about a week later, I heard that the master had passed on. At first, I did not associate his passing with anything in particular. However, I later realized that the day and time he passed on was the same day and time I had felt the huge surge of energy at the wedding ceremony. I somehow felt that this was Master Luong Minh Dang's way of saying good-bye.

There was a period in the mid-1980s when I experienced premonitions. The premonitions were sporadic and accompanied by a pulsation throughout my body. It was as though my normal body pulse increased twenty fold at the beginning of or during major events. On one of the first instances, I awoke at about 3:00 a.m. with my body pulsating, accompanied by a vision just before I awoke of a commercial airliner on fire. When I was finally able to fall asleep again and eventually awoke several hours later, a commercial airline crash was described on the news the same way it occurred in my dream. In this first instance, I attributed my vision to coincidence.

Another instance was just before I awoke, when in my dream, I saw a man that I knew, a chemical salesman from whom I had bought goods. He was walking toward me from the business next door, saying my name. I owned a bakery business at this time, and in my dream, I was standing at my back door, getting some air and smoking a cigarette. When I was at work later that morning, at about 11:00 a.m., I was standing at the back door outside my business. Just as it had occurred in my dream, there was Mike the chemical salesman, walking toward me, saying my name. It was an instant replay of my dream. I was in awe, but not at first; I did not realize for several minutes that I was reliving a sequence of my dream.

However, what was even more interesting was the question: Why him? Why Mike the chemical salesman? Because of my dream, I began asking Mike personal questions to try to determine a reason for seeing him in my dream and subsequently in reality the next day. I did not tell Mike why I was becoming so personal. His son was in the Israeli military and was, I believe, stationed in Lebanon. There was an Israeli military barracks attacked with a car bomb in 1982, in Tyre, Lebanon, that I had heard about a day or two earlier. I wondered if Mike knew where his son was, and if the dream had anything to do with him. I asked him if he knew where his son was stationed, but he said he didn't know because of intelligence reasons. Nothing definitive was ever related to me regarding the dream that I could associate with any specific event. Not having a relationship with Mike, I do not know of any more significance to the dream unless something occurred that I was never made aware of.

There were numerous other events, such as major earthquakes and other disasters, for which I experienced premonitions. I never mentioned what had occurred to anyone until recently. I was very upset with the premonitions, and I was afraid to tell anyone about them. I suspect that this was another experience in my life I did not want to deal with; similar to my issues I had with existentialism.

Other unusual occurrences I have had and continue to experience are the following: quite frequently knowing when someone is going to call, finishing another person's sentence before he or she does, and having a sense about who people really are as individuals and, in many instances, knowing certain aspects and events of their past.

There was another time when I had an upper respiratory infection for two or three weeks and was taking two different types of antibiotics. The antibiotics seemed to help in the beginning, and when I was finished with the dosage I actually felt well, but not 100 percent. After about a week, I was worse again, and my doctor prescribed another round of antibiotics, about a week's supply. I was later coughing up blood for a few days, and by Saturday night, it had become worse. I called my doctor again, and he suggested that I go to the emergency room and said he would call ahead.

After blood work and a CT scan with contrast in the ER, the nurse said the ER doctor would be in to talk to me after they received the results from the radiology department. This was about an hour or so later, after the CT scan now 2:30 a.m., and we had arrived at the hospital at about 10:30 p.m. The doctor entered my room at about 3:30 a.m. and stated that I had a mass in the lower right lobe of my right lung. He said it did not look like pneumonia but rather like a tumor. He mentioned that it was an area almost the size of a golf ball, with prong-like lines shooting out from the perimeter of the mass. I asked, "What do we do now?" He said, "We are going to admit you for further testing." At that point, my wife was in tears. I, for whatever reason, maintained my composure, but not for long. I said to the doctor, "I do not want to die, but I am not afraid." At that point, I was composed, but after the doctor left the room, I became emotional. I said, "Pam, I love you." I then said, "Pam, I must finish my book before I die, if I am to die." The doctor said that on Monday or Tuesday I would likely have a bronchoscopy, a procedure in which a small amount of fluid is removed from the site of the mass for biopsy purposes. Because I have COPD, in addition to my internist, I have a pulmonologist, a lung specialist who would actually perform the bronchoscopy procedure. The physician Anthony S. Shen, M.D., Pulmonary and Critical Care Medicine, Missouri Baptist Medical Center, Dr. Shen, is so knowledgeable and so thorough I feel so comfortable with him.

It was about an hour and a half before I reached my room, and it was then close to 4:00 a.m. I told Pam to go home and get some sleep, and she finally left reluctantly for home. I could not sleep after hearing the news of a possible malignant tumor. While lying in bed, I simply could not fall asleep even after I was given Xanax. About 4:30 a.m., there was a problem with my IV tubing, and it had to be relocated to my other arm. At this time, I was on three different IV antibiotics. At about 6:00 a.m., I started drinking coffee and eating some animal crackers from the nurse's station. I was actually awake from about 9:00 a.m. on Saturday morning to about 4:00 a.m. on Monday morning. My pulmonologist arrived to see me at about 7:30 a.m. on Sunday, and he stated that he would schedule the bronchoscopy for Tuesday. He also said that there was a 95 percent chance that the mass was not malignant. After the doctor left my room, I did feel some relief.

I called Pam to tell her what the doctor had said, and she too was relieved. I asked that she bring my meditation cushion and my prayer rug when she returned to the hospital. That evening, before I attempted to go to sleep, I began meditating. I placed a folded sheet on the floor for my cushion to avoid it touching the hospital room floor. I assumed my half lotus position and began meditating. Within a minute or so I felt a tremendous sense of energy throughout my body. The energy was similar to what I sometimes experience during my daily meditation. However, this energy was so much more intense, and it continued to increase. I became concerned about this energy and what it meant. I said, "Oh God, what is happening to me?" I received almost an immediate answer; for whatever reason, I was receiving the positive energy from the other hospital patients. Some was the energy of the patients who were awake even at this hour; I was receiving positive energy because the negativity of their ego was not nearly as prominent due to their illness, and it was being suppressed. The positive energy from those patients who were asleep was even stronger. It was about 1:00 a.m. on Monday morning, and this immense wave of energy continued to increase.

As I was receiving this mammoth amount of energy, I somehow felt obliged to return the energy as a healing transfer to the patients from whom it came. I continued to meditate, transferring back to the other patients this enormous infusion of energy. Because of the energy's incredibly pleasurable feeling, it was difficult to stop meditating. I was relaxed and simultaneously exhilarated on such an elevated scale. Almost throughout the entire time I was meditating, which I would estimate to be about thirty to forty minutes, I experienced ineffable tears of joy. Sometimes there just are not words to describe certain experiences.

Thank God, my biopsy was negative, and I wondered if the energy I received in the hospital was related to the negative result of the test. I was able to return home on Wednesday with oral medication. The area in question was affected only by pneumonia, without any secondary issues.

For years now, I have been appreciative for what I have and possess, without taking very much for granted in my life. I feel that with meditation, I have gained a balance and vision for what is truly important. However, after my experience in the hospital, I now find an even greater appreciation and purpose for my existence. I also believe that others have gained a better understanding of purpose and existence relating to the following.

Because of a recent spiritual shift gradually and increasingly occurring within the past two decades to a greater awareness, some people in many areas of the planet appear to have experienced an increase in traditional values and spiritual growth. The elevation of positive values and spirituality may be responsible for the positive perceptual transformation occurring in society. About 3 percent of the population is now experiencing a higher level of consciousness related to religion, spirituality, traditional values, compassion, empathy or special events occurring in their life. This number relating to the 3 percent is based on the truth attained through kinesiology. We need this elevated awareness, whatever the percentage it may be. It is actually positive energy gained, and its emission to the planet and the universe, even at a low percentage, is exponential and critical for the earth's survival.

This positive energy of 3 percent will assist in facilitating and negating much of the negative energy from the populace. This doesn't mean that the majority of the population is not good; they are good, just not at the level of consciousness needed to sustain the planet from the negative energy, generated by the masses, some registering below the level of integrity. The small percentage of positive energy described does in fact negate and neutralize enough of the negative energy created that, in turn, can and will avert the planet's self-destruction.

I am certain we have all experienced an interesting phenomenon that occurs and can relate to a higher awareness. It is feeling better about ourselves when walking outside after a hard rain or a swim in the ocean; when being close to a waterfall or being in a rural area; or when taking a bath, all of which usually relax and make us feel better and invigorated. Some studies have been done regarding this phenomenon. The study of "negative ions," which are odorless, tasteless, and invisible molecules that we inhale in abundance in certain environments. What varies, depending where we are, is the amount of negative ions. Negative ions increase the flow of oxygen to the brain, resulting in higher alertness, decreased drowsiness, and more mental energy; at the same time, it also helps us to relax. I especially and personally have a certain way I take a bath, which is lying in the bathtub with the drain closed and the shower on, as hot as I can stand it. I am slouched in the tub, stretched out the length, with the back of my head touching the rim of the back of the tub. The shower water hits me just below my neck and extends to the rest of my body. I mention this because I find it even more relaxing than a regular shower or bath. I turn the lights down with just barely enough light to be able to see. I find I can solve problems, find answers to questions much more easily, and feel immensely refreshed afterward. It is due to the abundance of the negative ions created from the water. I actually believe my shower and bath combination enhances the phenomena.

Web MD Feature:
[Denise] [Mann] *"Negative Ions Create Positive Vibes"*
May 6, 2002

Over the past several years, I feel I have become much more sensitive and compassionate, and I judge others less. My compassion and sensitivity appear to continually grow on a daily basis. I find that I have more peace within myself, especially regarding negative issues that would normally be stressful for me but which now seem much more trite, insignificant, and almost irrelevant. I have found more peace and satisfaction in my life without the desire for more material. Material does not have the importance it once did for me. All material and power fulfillment we receive is truly in essence hollow and shallow gratification. My perception of life now is about a much greater awareness of all that is and what is truly important for peace and satisfaction on the planet. I can only conclude that the peace and understanding I have realized is strictly due to my keeping my mind open to the universe as God, as well as to my mediation, and the prayer I perform daily. I have gradually, over the years, felt more at peace and balanced, with an increased understanding of existentialism. Recently, however, it is as though a light bulb lit spontaneously in my head, enabling a stark higher realization—almost an absolute knowing— of truth, understanding, and purpose. I suspect that the best way to describe this feeling is that it is an extreme, remarkable, overwhelming, and elevated sense of peace and understanding regarding existence.

SECTION 8

Purpose of Existence

Chapter 21

Humanity's Sensitivity

L ife is truly a short span of physical existence. What are sixty, seventy, eighty, ninety, or more years in the design of things? What is even a life span of ninety years or more in relation to, say, five hundred years, two or three thousand years, or the age of the dinosaurs, and millions of years ago? Thinking in these terms, our life span is no more than a blink of an eye in the scheme of things. It is truly no more than realizing that one day, if we are fortunate enough to do so, we will awaken and be forty, sixty or seventy-five years old or older. Will we be satisfied with our lives at this juncture? Will we believe we have accomplished our life's goal, if we even had one? Will we have peace from within? Will this peace include an abundant amount of sensitivity and compassion for others and for ourselves? Will we feel that we have gained fulfillment in our lives? Will we or should we even care?

Have we ever thought about the people who have been gone for, say, five hundred years? Could those people have had the same thoughts about life, existence, and the scheme of things I referred to earlier? Imagine two people today talking about a scenario relating to existence, regarding others that have been gone for over five hundred years. Now, what about two people talking about us, five hundred years from the present, when we have been gone for almost five hundred years? Will they discuss the same subject and scenario regarding our truly short existence on the planet? The answer to all these questions, of course, is yes. How about our ancestors, who have now been gone for three or four generations? Could any of them have had the same thoughts we are discussing now? And then about three or four generations from now? Our grandchildren and great-grandchildren will perhaps discuss us.

Recently, I watched a documentary on television. The credits were mentioned, and then the film referenced the date: November 10, 2010. I had this sudden realization of fifty years earlier, November 10, 1960, and then fifty years later, November 10, 2060. Fifty years from the present, I would be 118 years old, but I do not think I will be here. Do we ever have the blatant awareness of our mortality? Do we realize and can we appreciate the stunning realization of the scenarios just described—that someday we will cease to exist on the planet, regardless of how we might feel now? With this realization, would it not be feasible for us to focus on truth—the truth of who we are, the truth of our desires, and the truth relating to life itself and what is truly important and meaningful for true happiness?

It is fortunate that most of us are not obsessed with the thought of ceasing to exist. Somehow, the brain maintains a mechanism that, for the most part, neutralizes this thought. The thought is typically not prevalent, except on the occasion of funerals, accidents, or near-death experiences, or upon reaching a very old age. I suspect this is good, provided that we do realize that life is a short existence and act in accordance with this understanding and realization. Acceptance of nonexistence is difficult, and we generally fear what we do not understand. It is frightening to some people, but with a heightened awareness, fear diminishes.

I believe that if we could rise to the awareness described earlier, then perhaps we would function differently. Some people, as they grow older, may mellow in how they react and conduct themselves, through self-discovery and gained wisdom, which perpetuates more peace from within. Some people may experience elevated awareness at a younger age and may find contentment much sooner than others. However, others may become much more draconian in their actions, with an enhanced egocentric attitude and may never find peace or evolve to true happiness. I refer to those who always seem to need something to do and something to engage their time rather than being alone and learning to understand the self and finding peace in their lives. It seems that those people do not relish the thought of being alone very often, if at all. They would rather be with someone, read, and watch television, bowl, play golf, go out to dinner, and so on to occupy their time. Those things, of course, are good and fine, but with limitations.

If we feel that we have enough peace and happiness in our lives but that we still need more material, or more interludes that are romantic, more activities or more of this or more of that, then in all probability, we do not have true peace. The relentless search and the need for more material and different romantic affairs are immediate but hollow gratification, as discussed earlier. The true peace I refer to is obvious, and it is meaningful and sustainable. True peace would actually include the emotions of love and happiness, realized automatically when one finds true peace. True peace is the category of peace that is gained and sustained through learning about oneself. It would also include the subsequent application of sensitivity to and understanding of others through one's newly realized awareness. This new consciousness is not related to material things, and it is sustainable—a different brand of wealth and power that cannot be lost or taken away from us by anyone.

It may seem to some that needing that level of sensitivity and understanding to find peace is unnecessary and foolish. Many individuals do not believe there is a need for personal or spiritual growth. However, lacking an abundance of these attributes impedes our ability to find true peace in our lives, regardless of the level of monetary wealth and power we have. Many do not understand this. They believe that their current level of compassion and understanding is sufficient, and they likely have not even thought about improvement or change. In fact, they may feel somehow that to extend any more compassion and sensitivity to others may show an element of weakness, through which others will capitalize on their generosity and kindness. I believe that this assumption is fallacious and may merely be a justification by those who are simply not willing to improve their levels of positive emotions—or they may actually believe they do not need or want improvement. One's perception plays a significant role in this belief. How we perceive others can be negative to some and positive to others, meaning that perception is in the eyes of the beholder. In life, it is not what we see but rather how we see it. But the lack of a higher degree of emotion and sensitivity leads to our inability to recognize the importance of a truly meaningful existence—an existence without the struggle for more.

Greater emotion and sensitivity comes with the realization of a higher awareness.

We regularly need periods of time for self-introspection without the substitution of companionship or activities to avoid being alone.

This alone time will improve us as people and will allow us time to contemplate our lives, our true desires, values, spirituality, and the status of our evolution in becoming better individuals and better human beings and finding exact and true peace. I believe that exact and true peace brings both inner and external tranquility, balance, and harmony that are obtainable and sustainable.

True peace maintains strength and calm in the face of discord and tension.

The continual need for activities may be approximating occupational therapy. Just as we may do something immediately to take our mind off a particular issue or argument, which may include cleaning our home or exercising to forget and to relieve our stress. So do we feel as though we need to be doing something or we will be bored? Is it truly boredom we wish to avoid, or do we not want to face certain truths about ourselves? It is as though we must occupy our time to avoid thinking about ourselves and evolving as people, not being mindful of the growth that awaits us in understanding ourselves. Perhaps the reason we do not want to face truth about ourselves is that we may find that truth uncomfortable or distressing. The truths may relate to negative aspects of our lives and emotions or to idiosyncrasies that we do not want to recognize and deal with to promote self-improvement. We may not want to address certain aspects of ourselves because of negative emotions and perceptions we maintain about our lives and our realities. We may sometimes delude ourselves, avoiding alone time and circumventing the truth about ourselves. We may persist in deliberate evasion of the conscious and subconscious truths in our lives.

When we take classes in school, regardless of the subject, we attend lectures and must study at some point. When we purchase items that require us to read instructions to operate them, we usually do so.

Virtually everything in life that we purchase has some sort of a manual or basic instruction list or ingredients list. Why do we, then, assume that we know ourselves without studying ourselves? We become aware of different ways to operate as people, realizing our different personal ingredients or what we could achieve, qualities we might never have known that we possessed. Alone time and study of ourselves will improve us as people; this will be a time for us to contemplate our lives, our true desires, values, and spirituality, and our evolution in becoming better and fulfilled individuals. Facing the truth may be uncomfortable in the beginning, but it will ultimately set us free from inhibitions we may or may not be aware of, and it will enable us to find true peace and happiness.

We as younger people may substitute activities to avoid thinking about aspects of ourselves. The fact that some of us are older may make us feel not as productive, or there may be thoughts about life or emotions that we may not want to deal with. The activities become a substitute for these concerns.

In a sense, the activities become a diversion, but not in the same sense described in (Section 7, Energy.) The diversion then was to facilitate a release from negative thoughts or past situations. In this instance, though, the sustained activities are a deliberate attempt to avoid the truth. In addition, the activities facilitate for us a sense of more productivity, fulfillment, and reward—a sense that we are accomplishing something, even though the accomplishment may actually represent a shallow satisfaction. These may be activities such as improving our golf game by a few strokes or getting higher scores in our bowling, obtaining immediate gratification as a substitute for being alone. Again, activities are wonderful ways to supplement our time, with limitations. This would apply to anyone, whether a white-collar or blue-collar worker; or retired, alone time is necessary to establish development in the individual.

If you are interested in meditation, which is excellent for alone time, then please refer to Section 3, Meditation. The alone time I describe may be daily or intermittent, for a minimum of three times a week, and from twenty minutes to one hour or more. Evolution in our lives will allow us to establish better understanding of ourselves and will enable a higher degree of peace and satisfaction to surface. If you prefer something other than meditation, then sit on a sofa, on your most comfortable chair, or in whatever place you prefer. With your eyes open or closed, without distractions, permit your mind to be relaxed and open for whatever may enter. In addition, take three or four slow, deep breaths and remain in this position for a minimum of twenty minutes with a continually open, self-observed, calm mind. Alternatively, take a walk alone in the park or in a place that is quiet and only alive with nature. Observe nature, a tree, a branch, a rolling hillside, a flower, a bird, and the natural beauty and the sounds that exist within nature. Then you will discover the astonishing treasures that exist and can never be taken away from you by anything or anybody. Engaging in this type of solitude and introspective thought on a regular basis will ultimately perpetuate the evolution of a robust understanding of oneself and will ultimately provide an improved understanding of life and spirituality.

A person mentioned to me recently that it did not seem fair that we were born to die. For most of us, the gift of life gives us pleasure and degrees of happiness. But then we must leave the planet and all that we love and enjoy. I replied, "It is not the end but rather the beginning of a new existence." That is why it is imperative to grasp the understanding of how precious and short life is and to live your life with this understanding. If individuals could seize upon and understand how precious and short life is, perhaps then there would be an increased level of decency and integrity on the planet and greater peace for us all.

But it seems as though when we are younger, we have the sense that we are invincible. We know that we can die and can be harmed but simultaneously believe that it will not happen to us. As we grow older, we begin to realize that our physical vulnerability, and harm could occur to us and be much more possible than we previously thought. Some of us who are younger—and some of us as we grow older—may be fortunate enough to take a hard look at our lives and determine whether we are satisfied with our existence so far. Have we contributed to anyone or anything other than ourselves? Do we feel that what we have accomplished so far in life is sufficient? Do we even care? I say "fortunate enough," but I actually mean do we have, or have we realized, the level of consciousness required to understand what is truly important while we are here on the planet? If we could only recognize and appreciate the very limited physical time on earth we have, regardless of our age, perhaps we might have an acute awareness of its importance.

I have always searched for something in life beyond the material, more of a purpose and meaning regarding who we are and why we are here (existentialism). My wife and I enjoy and appreciate our home, cars, and other material things, but I always wanted my life to have more meaning and value than merely the acquisition of those things. Generally, when we desire more, we seek more material things, but we should in fact attempt to seek things that are more nonmaterial. We then may conduct our lives in a different manner, searching for and finding an enhanced understanding of our purpose. We then may not be disappointed and find that we perhaps have not achieved "playing our music" when it is our time to leave this life. In living our life's passion, we as individuals are playing our music.

For fulfillment of our lives, it is vital to have an understanding and appreciation of how precious and short life is. Perhaps then we would have less jealously, selfishness, envy, greed, and hostility on the planet. We would then realize that inner peace derives from conveying to others more compassion, sensitivity, and understanding rather than judgment. We must recognize the necessity for emotional self-nourishment, and we must overcome the questionable characteristics of the ideology and the sometimes-obscured reality of and by our society.

What is it that causes some of us to be less sensitive and less compassionate to others? Does less compassion and sensitivity perpetuate the different levels of consciousness we maintain? Was it our initial environments, parental relationships, and personal associations that contributed to the degree of sensitivity and compassion we maintain? Or is the reason the lower baseline we may retain of the level of consciousness we were born with, as described in Section 1? Is it our desire for money and power? Why do some of us lack a higher degree of sensitivity and compassion? Why do some of us have a higher level of sensitivity and compassion in our lives compared with others? Why do some of us have more concern about others' feelings?

Why do some care about their neighbors while others do not? Why do some care about what is happening in the world while others do not? What constitutes a caring person? What enables someone to say he or she is a good person? Do we feel we are good people? If we feel we are good people while others do not, which perception is correct—theirs or ours? Can we be truly objective in personal evaluations of who we are? We must also recognize that there is a need for improvement before we take action. This recognition is sometimes difficult to admit to ourselves—that we need development or change. Again, the type of development and change I am referring to is ego reduction. If you feel honestly and truly that you are completely happy with your life and that there is nothing that you would like to improve or feel better about, that is wonderful!

Chapter 22

Perception and Existence

One perspective can be completely different from another. Perception will eventually affect our attitude regarding others and even life itself. How we may perceive a person based on previous engagements may change. We should not necessarily hold the opinions we have about a person today to be true; they may be significantly different in later years. What we may perceive about an individual can determine how we act and feel. What we may see from one side of a room may be completely different from the other side. The moon is above the earth from the position at which we view the moon. Yet where is the moon's position from, say, the planets Venus or Mars? The position of the moon then is very different; it is no longer above the earth. What we may view from one side of the street would be very different from what we see on the other. What we may see about what kind of a person one is may be viewed completely the opposite way by another.

Perception is the key ingredient in our observations and sometimes in our understanding of a person or of situations. The accuracy of a subject may only be relative from the individual perception. Habit and tradition can obscure our perceptions of truth and of life's purpose and meaning. Ingredients that play a role in perception are parental indoctrination, the total overall environment, education, influential individuals, and personal discernment. All of these things help to perpetuate an attitude that in turn plays a significant role in our perceptions and ultimate performance. Perception can be essential in the assessment of some truths. However, if in truth it is our own perception, which then is relative to our individual assessment rather than authenticity, then what we consider truth may be a fallacious assumption. So how does one determine truth?

If possible, conclusions about the truth of a given situation or person should be derived from a compliance with reality, from the veracity of statements, and from verified, unquestionable facts. But can perception have such specificity? I think not. (Please refer to Section 6, Time, regarding integrity.)

Perception is the process of attaining, organizing, and interpreting sensory information and intuitive thought. So perception, because it is relative to the individual, may not provide an actual realization of that which we are attempting to distinguish. However, perception does play a key role in one's attitude toward others and toward life. How one perceives others and his or her own life contributes significantly to the individual's perceptual performance. I feel that in the pursuit of truth, it is logical and prudent to believe that veracity and fact are the primary determinants, with perception secondary.

Perception also plays a key role in various situations regarding our interpretations in life.

How truly insignificant are grudges, hate, and reprisals, and the sadistic satisfaction one may receive from these negative emotions.

Most people do not understand that negative emotions directed to others do harm to the donor rather than to the intended recipients. Stress may perpetuate anger or irritability, the by-products of which can be anxiety and, ultimately, depression. The anger, hatred, and disdain, if they are sustained, are cancerous emotions that eventually do enormous harm to the donor, mentally and physically.

To find pity shall enable forgiveness to surface.

The previous statement emphasizes the importance of recognizing dysfunction, of realizing and releasing one's negative posture of judgment and disdain. If we were unable to find forgiveness for someone through rationalization, then positive understanding, recognition, and acceptance of the situation because of the individual's ignorance would enable a road to pity. This involves recognition, realization, and justification of a disagreement or an action by another individual who is understood by us to be ignorant regarding a certain event. This will facilitate and enable pity to surface. Finding pity ultimately breeds forgiveness and will free us from the captivity of the negative chains that may imprison us.

When we are considering our desires, all that one may desire—love, peace, and joy—is already here and available to us all, but these emotions are obscured through the negative aspects of our egos. When it is an overcast day, we might say, "The sun is not out today." However, the sun is always out; it is simply obscured by the clouds. The same principle applies to love, peace, and joy, obscured by our ego. The existence of egocentric and negative attitudes may suppress or obscure our ability to achieve and maintain positive attitudes toward others and at times toward ourselves. But we need only open our minds and hearts and focus on eliminating or reducing any egoist feelings such as selfishness, jealously, envy, greed, hatred, or the fear of loss, which will then facilitate the love, peace, and joy we so deserve to surface. The fear of loss I refer to may relate to loss of material things or to the loss of life. Think about these negative emotions and how they may affect our lives. The greater the degree of the negative emotions we maintain, the more difficult it is for us to find the love, peace, and joy that already exists. Are we aware of the degree of these emotions that we maintain? Note what we as individuals think of in the course of a day, what we say to others, and how we act in daily our lives. Are our thoughts positive or negative about others and ourselves?

Ralph Waldo Emerson said that "*the ancestor of every action is a thought.*" In my opinion, it is important to recognize that one cannot take a break from time; it does not stand still. We must enable positive actions derived from our thoughts to survive. We should not permit procrastination, which is one of the ego's lieutenants who intervenes and attempts to circumvent the fulfillment of the thought.

Time is truly of the essence, and we must consider the importance of taking action to achieve that which we desire. Achievement is fulfillment and satisfaction that ultimately enriches our lives and brings to us a peace and happiness that we may then realize. Peace and happiness are what have always been available, but they are not always easily achieved. They will continue to remain attainable with the appropriate attitude and approach. We must act on as many positive thoughts as possible. In addition, we must also understand and prioritize that which is actually truly important to us and take action.

Chapter 23

Purpose and True Happiness

There were times when I was sailing in open water, out of sight of land, under sail without the auxiliary diesel engine operating, very quiet, with no engine, just the sails and the wind through nature moving us along. During the day, at different times, I could find myself in an involuntary trancelike state. This was particularly true on a clear night, with no backscatter of city lights to impede the truly awesome, unbelievable beauty of the heavens. I saw the stars and constellations like I'd never seen them before. They were so bright and so clear and seemed so close, yet were so far. Looking up into the heavens, I would sometimes feel a different type of trancelike state of mind. I did not feel the transfixed sense but rather had a feeling of the cosmos drawing me in. It was almost a feeling as though that may have been my home at one time. I felt as if I belonged there. It perpetuated an extremely joyous and peaceful sense about me. It felt so comfortable, so true. I just felt so good about myself, so happy, so vibrant, and so alive. I almost felt as one with the universe. For the period of time this state of mind lasted, I knew no yesterday or tomorrow; I only knew the enhanced presence.

Have you ever felt the way I just described? You do not necessarily need to feel that you are one with the universe but rather just feel so good about yourself, so vibrant, so happy, and so good to be alive. It is a euphoric feeling. During this time of joy, you feel so uninhibited that you actually simply experience the purity and the essence of happiness. You feel so unbelievably good that you do not want it to end. It does usually end, but it does not always need to end. If you have never felt this way before, you must find a way to feel like this and experience pure joy; it is the most astonishing, intoxicating state of mind. If you have experienced this degree of happiness before, it can occur again more frequently and for longer durations. It is truly a natural high; I believe you are actually high on life itself.

The kind of happiness described above is not sustainable forever; however, maintaining this type of happiness is attainable much more frequently and for longer durations then we may realize. It is still all about reducing the negative aspects of our egos. Obviously, there are times in our lives when frustration and discord may be prevalent, inhibiting our ability to maintain the purity of true happiness. Therefore, the idea of 100 percent sustained happiness is not realistic. The individual's ability to achieve ego reduction determines the degree of happiness and duration within the person. It is important to understand the negative aspects of our daily lives, including the role the ego plays overall in our lives and in the reduction of our negativity.

It is very possible to be happier more often than not. If we are being truly honest with ourselves without deluding our true feelings, are we happy more often than not? Does life seem sad, so that we are not happy a good percentage of the time, or are we just OK, or are we generally aggravated or irritable? Life does not have to be this way. The degree of true happiness for an individual can improve regardless of where one might be on the scale.

In order to find true happiness, one must focus on the release of judgment and must pursue the acquisition of more understanding with regard to others and oneself. In addition, ego reduction of the primary negatives—selfishness, jealousy, envy, greed, the fear of loss, fear itself, and hatred—will facilitate the emergence of a new and more sustained happiness. The dramatic reduction of these negative emotions is imperative to enable true happiness to surface. If you truly have a desire to gain more sustained happiness, peace, and contentment in your life, then consider reducing the negative aspects of your ego.

I believe it is fear, doubt, and the remaining ego that inhibit and obstruct our ability to find higher levels of compassion, understanding, peace, and integrity in our lives. Fear inhibits our ability to understand; doubt inhibits our ability to trust; and our ego itself, emitting lower levels of integrity, hinders the emergence and acceptance of truth.

How can ego reduction be attained in one's life? Evaluation of truthfulness, compassion, and tolerance of every thought, word, and deed would be ideal. However, such idealism is easy to state but rather difficult to achieve. One must think about one's posture and take some time to do *self-analysis* when the primary ego negatives of selfishness, jealousy, envy, greed, the fear of loss, fear itself, and hatred arise. Be cognizant of how you act and respond to other people and situations. To begin with, simple material things such as clothing and jewelry that we buy and wear can induce ego. Realize that buying or wearing a piece of jewelry, a wristwatch, or clothing meant to *impress* someone is ego. However, an individual wearing something because he or she likes it and desires to do so to please himself or herself is ego reduction. This would apply to anything material. In addition, refraining from any attempts to impress anyone may aid in ego reduction. This includes what one states verbally or how one performs daily. Humble *subtlety* or *nuance* is a road to ego reduction. Feeling *superiority* over others is a companion to ego. We must find *sensitivity, understanding, compassion,* and *tolerance* and must reduce or eliminate the possible *humiliation* and *ridicule* of others. We should think about our actions before we take them. Consider how you would like to be treated, and how you as an individual would prefer being addressed. Do not take advantage of another's passive demeanor.

Realize that the seven negative egoist examples of, selfishness, jealousy, envy, greed, the fear of loss, fear itself and hatred are emotions and a means of treatment that we would not be fond of receiving ourselves. That should provide justification for us not to give negative treatment to others, unless we continue to seek superiority. Perception plays a key role in our demeanor and our behavior. Do you remember the expressions "count to ten before you speak" or "take two or three deep breaths before you take action?" To achieve a higher degree of happiness and ego reduction, it is beneficial to think about our actions before we initiate them. If we truly have a desire to raise our levels of consciousness, we must take action to change who we are through ego reduction. The truth of our identities as individuals is obscured by the duality created by our perceptions, but this obscuring will ultimately disappear with the release of as many egoist negative beliefs and attitudes as possible. Total ego elimination is not probable in the normal daily existence that we know, but significant reduction is.

I recall sitting on our patio in the rear of our condominium early one summer evening, sipping a glass of my favorite red wine. My wife was inside, doing something about dinner preparation. The sun was shining, and it was about 82 degrees. There were just a few Cumulus clouds, and the remainder of the sky was a deep, bright blue. The humidity was low, and the air just felt so wonderful. I was sitting at a small umbrella table, very comfortably soaking up the day. The common area here is so beautiful, with a couple of rolling hills and the association swimming pool just behind us, about one hundred feet away, elevated slightly on its own perch. The pool can be a bit noisy on the weekends, but this was during the week, and it was quiet. The area is about thirty years old, as one can realize from the size of the tree trunks. The grass is cut every Wednesday, and it looks like a plush green carpet. My head was slightly tilted back as I looked at the tree branches above me. I was thinking of the utter complexity, yet perfection of nature and life, and I felt so happy, so alive, so good about myself. Then I experienced the distinctive, blatant vibrancy of my reality at this moment, and an unmistakable pure awareness inhabited my being.

Everything that exists already exists in a state of true perfection. I had this feeling of an enhanced clarity of realism that was so awe-inspiring. I was truly not only in the moment but was also beyond the moment, in an original sort of elevated presence or an enhanced reality. I had clarity of the present moment far beyond our normal awareness. Probably the best way to describe it would be in terms of a deeper dimension. Our reality, of course, has three dimensions: height, width, and depth. I use the idea of a deeper dimension in an attempt to describe an even greater degree of clarity of reality as I saw and felt it at the time.

The entire experience lasted about a minute, and then the vibrant sense I experienced was gone. I again felt so blessed to have experienced this incredible moment. If I could only have sustained this incredible time throughout my life! If we could only sustain this vibrant type of moment through all of our time we spend on the planet, what a different perception of life would prevail. I have found a greater degree of love, peace, and joy within the past five years. I believe it is due to my intense desire for more of an awareness and meaning for life.

On a Sunday afternoon in August 2011, my wife and I were taking a walk in the beautiful St. Louis Botanical Garden, a national landmark with seventy-nine acres of scenic landscaping and historic structures. The Botanical Garden, also known as Shaw's Garden of St. Louis, features plants from around the world. The garden is in a unique setting and was founded and created back in 1859 by Henry Shaw, an English immigrant and entrepreneur.

There are many areas in the garden with fountains, many of which are used for wishing wells. It was a beautiful, sunny, clear afternoon, with the temperature at about 89 degrees. We approached one of the fountains, and I took two coins from my pocket, giving one to Pam and keeping the other. She made her wish and tossed the coin into the fountain. I was always searching in my life for something. I would normally wish that I would find what I was looking for in my life or find someone to love and be loved by in return. Both of those wishes had been fulfilled. I began to make a wish and had the most extraordinary, surprising awareness: I could not think of a wish. For the past several years, I have felt very content with my life but never had this stark awareness until that moment. I had a blatant, astonished realization that my desires were in fact fulfilled, and I could not think of anything that I wanted to wish for that was not already in my life. How blessed I felt, with this now obvious and deliberate awareness of total fulfillment! I said at the time, "Thank you, oh God, for all that I have and for all that is."

"Life finds it purpose and fulfillment
in the expansion of happiness"
—Maharishi

It is my belief that the sole purpose of existence is to enjoy life to its fullest and to obtain ultimate degrees of love, peace, and joy through whatever path this discovery may take us, provided that it does not harm anyone else. This *will* generate enriched happiness! This, I believe, is the exclusive purpose of our lives, of our existence. We all maintain free will, hence our ability to choose our paths even though initially they may not be correct. This is our truth and our authenticity. One must find the ability to recognize the fundamental and moral beliefs one knows are true, those that may be concealed deep in the foundation of one's heart or soul. Establish and follow your passion for work, for a job you know you would love to do. When you find your passion, I believe you will be doing a job that does not seem like work. Trust in God, trust in yourself, and work hard at that which is your passion, changing course at times, if necessary, to attain your goal. With the unquestionable recognition of your heart's desire and the unadulterated fervor and determination for achievement, success and satisfaction are indisputably in the very near future.

Love, peace, and joy are life's purpose, which enables true happiness to surface. When this is enhanced and coupled with our passion for work, we will rise to the ultimate form of true happiness on the planet. There is just simply nothing else that would indicate any further purpose to life. To ask or probe further involves the same futility as asking why a dog chases its tail. Why is there space? It simply is. Why is there life? God's creation simply is. Why are there stars and planets? They simply are. Everything in the universe is already truly in a state of exquisite perfection, and so will life be as well, when one enables true happiness to surface.

For many years, I searched for more of a purpose and a meaning to life and existence. I was always looking for external, materialistic solutions. But the material things never seemed to satisfy me; I always repeatedly searched for more. I continually believed and relentlessly pursued, and I felt that there was something more significant to my existence. I believed I needed to evolve to something, perhaps with more reason or more awareness and more purpose to my life and myself. I finally realized, through new realizations and after much time and meditative thought, that it was love, peace, and joy that were missing from my life. Hence, I now know what is the necessary foundation for achieving purpose and meaning when it comes to life and existence, which ultimately breeds the epitome of fulfillment. It was the love of myself and the love of another that was lacking. I found that peace ultimately derived from finding love and that joy derived from finding peace.

I sincerely wish that the reader has gained a better understanding and appreciation of life's purpose and meaning. May your life become more enriched, and may you find a deeper peace in a fulfilled existence.

May God grant that all of you who
seek true happiness find true happiness.

Summary of Purpose and True Happiness

1) What is a lifetime of even ninety years or more in relation to, say, two or three thousand years?

2) Thinking in these terms, our life spans are no more than a blink of an eye.

3) Will we be satisfied with our lives at a later juncture?

4) Will we have peace from within? Will this peace include an abundant amount of sensitivity and compassion for others and for ourselves?

5) True peace includes happiness, and it is obvious, meaningful, and sustainable.

6) True peace is the category of peace gained and sustained through learning about oneself through a newly realized awareness.

7) This new consciousness is nonmaterial-related, and it is sustainable. It is a different brand of wealth and power that cannot be lost or taken away by anyone.

8) The lack of sensitivity and understanding impedes our ability to find and have true peace in our lives, with or without the existence of monetary wealth and power.

9)   When people lack the desire for increased awareness and don't recognize the need for improvement, this affects their ability to achieve growth, greater peace, and happiness.

10) Refusing to extend more compassion and sensitivity to others may stem from weakness or from a belief that others will capitalize on one's generosity and kindness. This belief is almost always false. The assumption of this position is usually mere justification by people who are simply not willing to improve their levels of positive emotions.

11) One's perception plays a significant role in the earlier beliefs.

12) How we perceive others can be negative to some and positive to others, hence, perception is in the eyes of the beholder.

13) In life it is not what we see, but rather how we see it.

14) The lack of a higher degree of emotion and sensitivity produces our inability to recognize the importance of a truly meaningful existence.

15) Have we ever thought about people who have been gone for over five hundred years? Could those people have had the same thoughts we have about life, existence, and the scheme of things?

16) Do we ever have the blatant awareness of our mortality, recognizing that someday we will cease to exist on the planet, regardless of how we might feel now?

17) With this realization, would it not be conceivable and feasible for us to focus on truth: who we are and the truth of our desires, the truth relating to life itself, and what is truly important and meaningful for true happiness?

18) We do not relish the thought of being alone very often or at all.

19) Alone time will improve us as people; this is a time for us to contemplate our lives, our true desires, values, and spirituality and our evolution in becoming better people and finding exact and true peace.

20) True peace maintains strength and calm in the face of discord and tension.

21) Do we avoid alone time to avoid facing the truths about ourselves? We may at times delude ourselves, to avoid alone time and to evade the conscious and subconscious truths in our lives.

22) Alone time for us may be daily or one to three times a week, for about twenty minutes to one hour.

23) What one does in alone time may be meditation or simply introspective thought in a place without distractions.

24) Seize and understand how precious and short life is; then we will have an increased level of decency, integrity, and peace on the planet.

25) Have we contributed to anyone or anything other than ourselves? Do we feel that what we have accomplished so far in life is sufficient?

26) Have an acute awareness of life's importance and its impermanence.

27) Seek more nonmaterial values rather than material.

28) Was it our initial environment, parental relationships, or personal associations that have contributed to the degree of sensitivity and compassion we maintain?

29) We must recognize that there is a need for improvement before we take action.

30) Perception will eventually affect our attitudes about others and even about life itself.

31) Habit and tradition can obscure our perceptions of truth and of life's purpose and meaning.

32) Although perception is important in the pursuit of truth, it is logical and prudent to believe that veracity and fact are the primary determinants.

33) Extending pardon through rationalization, positive understanding, recognition, and acceptance of the situation because of the individual's ignorance would enable a road to pity and ultimately to forgiveness.

34) What we desire is already here, but it is obscured by negative aspects of our egos.

35) Time is of the essence, and one must consider the importance of taking action to achieve that which one desires.

36) Act on as many positive thoughts as possible, prioritizing by importance.

37) Happiness can be sustained for longer durations.

38) Ego reduction will determine the degree of happiness and its duration within the person.

39) The degree of true happiness experienced by an individual can improve, regardless of where he or she might be on the scale.

40) Significant reduction of judgment, selfishness, jealousy, envy, greed, hatred, fear of loss, and fear itself will ultimately facilitate the emergence of a new and more sustained happiness.

41) Fear, doubt, and the remaining ego inhibit and obstruct our ability to find higher levels of compassion, understanding, peace, and integrity in our lives.

42) Ego reduction requires self-analysis.

43) Be cognizant of how you act and respond to other people and situations.

44) Wearing or utilizing material items to impress others is, in fact, ego.

45) Humble subtlety is a road to ego reduction, but intended or unintended superiority to others is a companion to ego. Learn to discover sensitivity, understanding, compassion, and tolerance, and reduce or eliminate any humiliation and ridicule of others.

46) All that exists is already in a state of true perfection.

47) Find and recognize the fundamental and moral beliefs you know are true and which are embedded in your heart and soul.

Afterword

In the past several years, I find my life to be far more at peace, with a greater awareness and understanding of purpose and what is truly important in our existence. I have realized that life will emanate true happiness for us when we understand humankind rather than judge it. With this consciousness, we can overcome negative emotions such as hate, humiliation, and destruction, ultimately transcending them to find love, peace, and joy. With this *understanding of understanding*, we will then be on a road to a collective peace that permeates the entire planet's population.

המציל נפש אחת, כאילו הציל עולם מלא

"Whoever saves one life, saves the entire world"

* * *

The Talmud, the Jewish sacred text of oral law and tradition, teaches us Adam was created in the beginning, as a single human being and he was the entire human population of the world at that time. In the same respect, we need to look at each individual as if he or she were the entire population of the planet. Hence, when you save one life it is as if you saved the entire world.

Talmud, Sanhedrin 37a states:

"FOR THIS REASON WAS MAN CREATED ALONE, TO TEACH THEE THAT WHOSOEVER DESTROYS A SINGLE SOUL... SCRIPTURE IMPUTES [GUILT] TO HIM AS THOUGH HE HAD DESTROYED A COMPLETE WORLD; AND WHOSOEVER PRESERVES A SINGLE SOUL. SCRIPTURE ASCRIBES [MERIT] TO HIM AS THOUGH HE HAD PRESERVED A COMPLETE WORLD."

Quotations from

"THE STRENGTH IN KNOWING"

***

*CONVEY TO OTHERS MORE COMPASSION, SENSITIVITY,
UNDERSTANDING RATHER THAN JUDGEMENTALISM"*

TO FIND PITY SHALL ENABLE FORGIVENESS TO SURFACE

*THERE ARE GOOD BONES IN EVERYONE'S BODY, WHAT
VARIES ARE THE NUMBER*

*CAUSE AND EFFECT FROM THE VERY SMALLEST ACT BY ONE
INDIVIDUAL CAN CHANGE MANKIND FOR ALL TIME*

DEVASTATION CAN BE A REWARD, AND A PATH TO REGENERATION

EMOTIONS MAY INHIBIT OUR ABILITY TO FIND PEACE

ONE MUST CONQUER ONE'S INSENSITIVITY TO SENSITIVITY

*TRUE PEACE MAINTAINS STRENGTH AND CALM IN THE FACE OF
DISCORD AND TENSION*

WISDOM IS NOT GURANTEED TO BE ACHIEVED WITH AGE BUT RATHER REALIZED WITH ONES SENSITIVIY TO MAN AND THE UNIVERSE

OPPOSITES CREATE DUALITY. THE EGO CREATES OPPOSITES. THEREFORE, THE EGO CREATES DUALITY

ONE SHOULD NOT PERMIT HIS OR HER LIFE PATH TO BE INFLUENCED BY THE EXPECTATIONS OF OTHERS.

DOUBT IS THE ARCHENEMY OF THE PURITY OF THOUGHT AND IT INHIBITS THE ESSENCE OF ALL THAT IS

OUR, EMOTIONS AND PERCEPTIONS DETERMINE OUR ATTITUDES AND ULTIMATELY OUR CHOICES

DON'T DO IT LATER; DO IT NOW.

TRUE LOVE IS UNCONDITIONAL AND EVERLASTING AND IT CANNOT CEASE.

REFRAMING FROM NEGATIVE SPEECH IS A PATH TO REDUCTION OF NEGATIVE THOUGHT

UNCONTAMINATED UNDERSTANDING AND AWARENESS IS THE PURITY OF ESSENCE AND THE ESSENCE OF PURITY

About the Author

I Alan Appt currently resides in the Midwest of the USA. He lives with Pam, his beautiful wife; Murphy, the very lovable cat; and Dolly, the vocal yellow-naped Amazon parrot. He has an adult daughter and son, as well as a grandchild.

Appt's childhood involved much philosophical thinking that has enabled a heightened, self-observing consciousness throughout his life. His book conveys his awareness, gentle demeanor, sensitivity, and deep insights.

After and education at the School of Human Universal Energy and Spirituality (HUESA), under the guidance of Master Luong Minh Dang, Appt became a teacher and a Master of Universal Energy. Over the past two decades, he has taught and practiced intense meditation daily. He has extensively studied kinesiology, a muscle-testing technique for determining truth. Appt is a retired United States Coast Guard licensed Captain who owned and operated a sailing charter business for six years on the west coast of Florida. He is also an accomplished Impressionistic artist painting in oils with the sole use of palette knives. Appt is currently a spiritual counselor, motivational speaker, and an ordained interfaith minister.

For further information regarding speaking engagements or questions, please contact I. Alan Appt through his website:

www.ialanappt.com

Made in the USA
Lexington, KY
16 June 2017